GRAVE CONCERNS

Locating and Unearthing Human Bodies

Kathryn Powell PhD

www.
AUSTRALIANACADEMIC**PRESS**
.com.au

First published in 2010
Australian Academic Press
32 Jeays Street
Bowen Hills Qld 4006
Australia
www.australianacademicpress.com.au

National Library of Australia Cataloguing-in-Publication entry

Author:	Powell, Kathryn.
Title:	Grave concerns : locating and unearthing human bodies / Kathryn Powell.
Edition:	1st ed.
ISBN:	9781921513701 (pbk.)
	9781921513718 (ebook)
Subjects:	Criminal investigation. Forensic anthropology. Human remains (Archaeology)
Dewey number:	363.25

Cover photograph by Roberta Blake. Cover design by Maria Biaggini.

Contents

Speechless beneath mounds and heaps of stones they lie, in lonely places upon airy mountain-sides, by rivers roaring swollen from the molten snows of springtime, and in leafy glens where only the wolf's whelp howls. They are mute beneath the greensward …

Nikolai Tolstoy, from *The Coming of the King*

Acknowledgments

Clandestine graves, as man-made structures in the environment, cross many areas of study, and during the development of this book I found myself speaking with a wide range of people; from geologists to technicians, to biologists, pilots, lawyers and soil scientists among others. I found at first some degree of mystification, curiosity and surprise at the topic, but this was followed by considerable interest, discussion and time given to explore various aspects of buried bodies and gravesites. Those people to whom I am most grateful are Professor Maciej Henneberg (University of Adelaide), Colin Rivers and others at Commonwealth Scientific and Industrial Research Organisation (CSIRO), Dr Graham Heinson (University of Adelaide), the guys from Ecophyte, Trevor Evans from Primary Industries and Resources South Australia (PIRSA). Detective Superintendent John Venditto of the South Australia Police (SAPOL) particularly facilitated the provision of information that was useful to this book, and was supportive of the concept. Mr Mick Draper of the University of Adelaide library was particularly patient and helpful with all my online searches and I extend my thanks. I would like to make special mention of Dr Walter Wood, who has given thoughtful feedback on drafts and encouraged me to write this book.

The Australia and New Zealand Forensic Science Society awarded me a travel fellowship that enabled me to gain valuable background material by meeting with colleagues in the United States and the United Kingdom. This was rewarding and precipitated the subsequent years of research.

Other friends and colleagues have helped to hone the presentation of the contents of this book by reviewing different sections, and I am especially grateful for their critique and encouragement.

My research on this subject was conducted over seven years, and was begun when my sons were quite young. The book took a further two years. We now have more than one computer and their mother's strange work now has a title.

Most especially I would like dedicate this book to my mother, Dorene, not because she has a special interest in this subject but because she invested her time in me.

1

Setting the Scene

Constructing graves is a uniquely human activity. Graves and their making are steeped in ritual and customs, and have been the subjects of scholarly study. There are several types of graves; those of the legendary (such as King Arthur), the historical and archaeological (such as Tutankhamen or Nefertiti), mass graves (those of the victims of tragedy, killed in conflicts and battles), and the many varieties of customary burials (past and present). The subject of this book is a different type of grave: that of clandestine graves, in which are buried ordinary citizens who are victims of foul play. The difficulties of searching for buried murder victims have been faced as long as clandestine graves have been used to conceal the act of murder. Well-known examples of hidden bodies include the Backpacker Murders in New South Wales, the Saddleworth Moors Murders in the United Kingdom, the Truro Murders in South Australia, and more recently, the still unresolved search for Peter Falconio in the Northern Territory.

This book has been written as a comprehensive source of information about contemporary buried human remains and how they are found. Buried human remains need to be recovered, because the body is the primary element of evidence (*corpus delicti*) demonstrating a murder has been committed. In the best-case scenario, there will be a successful prosecution of the murderer. For family and friends, it is about ascertaining the fate of the person they cared for and reclaiming them as part of their grieving process. Yet the subject of clandestine graves has received limited attention.

Clandestine graves are the results of criminal acts — both murder and the wrongful disposal of a body — and therefore as a practice they sit outside the normal activities of our secularised, contemporary, industrialised society. These earthen repositories are found all over the world, wherever murder occurs and attempts are made to conceal the act. As man-made sites, this book addresses the physical and cultural anthropology of clandestine graves, detailing their features and context. The clandestine grave is not the only way to dispose of a body that is now a liability to the perpetrator, but it is a method that continues to be used and one that requires less ingenuity than other more elaborate or creative means. You will read about where such graves are commonly found, what surface signs might be found at a clandestine gravesite, and what tools have been used to detect a buried body.

Burial of the dead has a long cultural history as a common practice of humankind and is thought to have begun between 100,000 and 40,000 years ago (Quigley, 1963). As a way of dealing with human remains, the burial method features in many different cultures, including the early Christians, ancient Greeks and early Australian Aboriginals, continuing during the Medieval age and through to modern times. Mortuary and funeral practices have been documented over a wide variety of cultures, and have provided a point of reflection about what practices associated with the dead say about the living (Metcalf & Huntington, 1991), including the study of changing caskets and burial chambers over time. Yet the practices associated with the preparation and construction of clandestine graves has not been the subject of historical, criminal or anthropological study.

A dead body has a story to tell, as many crime novels and television series have promoted. Across a wide spectrum of what is now known as forensic work, evidence is delivered to solve murders and wrong doings from white-collar crime to responsibilities for accidents (such as in the field of structural engineering). Centres to study the decomposition of bodies have been established and are the source of numerous popular interest stories (such as the 'body farm' in Tennessee, made famous through the novelist Patricia Cornwall).

My own interest in this area began when I was working for the South Australian police in 1998. Given the vast outback areas in Australia, and scrubland always close to and within major living areas, it is not surprising that police believed there to be many clandestine graves that were yet to be found. Although clandestine graves were accepted as phenomena, there had been little research in Australia or most other countries in the late 20th century. This is mainly because anthropological work on dead bodies came after they were found, but increasingly police had begun to draw on scientific expertise during investigations. The work of William Bass, an

American anthropologist well known for his foundation work on locating buried bodies and simulating burials (highlighted in Chapter 2), stood out as pioneering, and this gave me inspiration for what was to become the subject of seven years of research.

Introducing Science to Locating a Clandestine Grave

Bodies are difficult to completely destroy. Clandestine graves are not about the destruction of the body, but rather burial of the evidence (a murder victim) in order to mask a crime. Who is going to look for the body? Police are the lead agency in criminal matters, and while they are responsible for investigations, they now often include forensic anthropologists, archaeologists, soil scientists and geologists, among others, in searches for buried bodies.

The ways in which search techniques have developed and progressed is the subject of Chapter 2, in which significant research and trial-based approaches used during the late 20th century are described. There were a range of outcomes achieved in this developmental period; some successful, some giving ambiguous results, and others with poor results. The somewhat trial- and-error approach reflects circumstances in which dedicated professionals had limited opportunity to experiment or practise good science. The imperatives of the murder investigation do not usually provide that luxury.

Bones, burials and repeated behaviours are the stuff of anthropology, and anthropologists have played a key role in searches for buried bodies. Initially, requests for assistance from anthropologists in criminal investigations had been limited to bone identifications after remains had been found. From the 1980s, many anthropologists and archaeologists found themselves being asked to search for clandestine graves, at a time when there were few published case studies of forensic searches for graves or other specific source material. In the United States, Professor Jeffrey B. Schwartz (1993), a noted anthropologist, recalls the first time he had been engaged by police to actually lead the search for the victim's graves:

> This was a far cry from being asked to identify a bone that had already been found. For one thing, it is not a trivial feat to locate a grave that someone has sought to hide. The only experience I had had in trying to find isolated burials that were not in 'expected' places such as cemeteries was while on excavation … (p. 86)

Figure 1.1 is a photograph of an area in which the body of a murder victim was buried. Taken from crime files, it is a good example of what search teams are faced with when they begin.

FIGURE 1.1
Scene of a targeted search area for a buried murder victim, South Australia.
Source: SA Police, published with permission.

Not all gravesites are the same, and clandestine graves have fewer distinguishing characteristics compared with burials of historical and funeral styled rituals, and also the mass burials dug during political conflicts. Techniques used to locate these other kinds of unmarked graves were applied to locate the hidden graves of murder victims. Human remains in forensic clandestine graves are best detected without disturbing a crime scene, as excavation will alter the layout irreversibly. To this end, geophysical instruments have been applied as non-invasive methods for detecting subsurface anomalies. These have been used for some time by archaeologists for site detection, because of their capacity to identify subsurface anomalies (Fischer, 1980; Ebert, 1984; McManamon, 1984; Scollar, Tabbagh, Hesse, & Herzog, 1990; Hunter & Martin, 1996). Examples include ground penetrating radars, magnetometers and resistance meters. At this time, there is no purpose-developed instrument to detect human remains below the ground surface. This book describes evidence of the effectiveness of instruments more usually used to examine soil layering or locating pipelines, cables or even ordinance devices.

The Clandestine Grave as a Burial Environment

What do we know about clandestine graves? The gravesite is a man-made area that has had a new element added: the body, which changes the ecosystem both above and below ground level. To find a hidden body within its grave environment, we need to look at the degree of resilience of a landscape marred by a grave; its capacity to withstand such a disturbance, and to renew itself and return to its pre-disturbed state, or something new and distinctive. It is in the interests of the investigator that the landscape does not have a high degree of resilience so that anomalies and signs of disturbance can be more easily identified.

Chapters 3 and 4 take a close look at clandestine graves as unnatural phenomena. A spotlight is placed on the adaptive processes of the upper surface landscape, to identify signs of the interim changes as the landscape moves towards restoration. Chapter 3 describes the surface signs of a grave that follow ground disturbance. Some environments are more likely than others to show signs of having been disturbed (contrast a desert of sand with a suburban garden, for example), and will be responsive to weather conditions and other various physical forces. In Chapter 4, the focus is on what happens below the ground surface and what remains of the body under different conditions. The decomposition process and interaction between the body and the surrounding soil is described, paying attention to the factors that will impact on the rate of decomposition, such as clothing on the body, moisture, temperature and insect activity. These aspects will vary from burial to burial. What occurs beneath the soil will provide the basis for subsurface detection methods, as conditions depart from the original preburial state. In the end, human bones are the definitive indicator of the presence of a person. The bones clearly represent that a person existed and is now dead, and has been deliberately placed there.

Investigations

Clandestine graves and the bodies within are found either by accident (stumbled across) or through a concerted effort in an official missing persons investigation. The next few chapters outline the reality of where murder victims tend to be buried and how they are found. Bodies will be buried in environments that are accessible and offer perceived unobtrusive areas in which bodies can be hidden. Specific environmental landscapes will offer various kinds of burial opportunities.

In the United Kingdom, an analysis of 29 cases of clandestine grave body locations showed that burial depths were hurriedly dug with common garden instruments and were shallow (averaging 0.4 m). The locations of the graves varied from woodland areas to gardens, and beneath structures such as household floorboards (Hunter & Cox, 2005). Chapter 5 examines the types of environments in which bodies have been located by police in Australia. Faced with even a small area to investigate the possible or surmised presence of a body, it is alluring to overestimate the capacity of technology to correctly locate buried human remains. As in other parts of the world, subsurface anomaly detectors of various kinds, including ground-penetrating radar, have been applied but with mixed success. The irregular inclusion of subsurface instrumentation and the lack of funded research tends toward an ongoing trial-and-error approach to locating buried murder victims.

Simulating Clandestine Graves

Outside of actual investigations (or casework), experiments and research have been carried out to identify the characteristics of gravesites and to test the effectiveness of potential location methods. This has involved drawing on several disciplines, including anthropology (physical, biological and cultural), biology, geophysics, taphonomy, archaeology and geology (soil science). Some of these experiments have involved simulating clandestine burials. Several studies have now been carried out involving the burial of human cadavers or pigs to examine the topographical nature of graves and the effectiveness of location techniques (Rodriguez & Bass, 1985; Schultz, Falsetti, Collins, Koppenjan, & Warren, 2002; Freeland, Miller, Yoder, & Koppenjan, 2003; Powell, 2006). Such sites provide a realistic opportunity to examine aspects of burial and grave detection techniques. The observations and subsurface test results of a grave research site in a semi-arid setting are described in detail in Chapter 6. By describing the results of several years' observation of simulated clandestine graves, the above ground changes can be tracked sequentially. These sites also provided important data on various geophysical instruments, as they were used to survey these known graves.

There are significant ethical considerations in establishing research or simulated sites, the most well-known example being the 'body farm' in Tennessee. Obtaining bodies for scientific experiments must follow the procedures and permission processes relevant to each country and state within that country. There are also permission and legislative processes to adhere to regarding where bodies can be buried outside of designated cemetery areas. The bodies must be protected during the research phase. For example, it would be unethical to allow faunal scavenging to result in human bones being found outside of the research area. For these reasons pigs, which have a similar body mass to people, have most often been substituted for human bodies.

The Cultural Anthropology of Clandestine Graves

Hiding or interfering with a body is subject to legal penalties. Disposing of a body is not a straightforward or easy task. Despite the ultimate severe legal sanctions for murder, this act continues to be committed and victims continue to be hidden. Chapter 7 considers the contemporary context for murder and hiding of the body. What follows a murder is dependent on the perceived choices of the protagonist (the murderer). This section describes the various ways in which bodies have been hidden (e.g., bodies have been found cemented into wheelie bins), in terms of available environmental opportunities and the logistics involved.

From the pragmatic to the social, cultural assumptions and, in particular, beliefs associated with death and burial impact on human behaviour — what are these and what part do these play in the decision to hide a body? The broader social context is explored in this book as the backdrop for the use of clandestine graves and concealment of a body. This context must include recognition of the growing prominence and influence of the 'forensic' field, the parameters set through law for the disposal of bodies and consequences, and the way in which discoveries of hidden bodies are portrayed to the public.

At any given point, contemporary attitudes are influenced by the collective past of a society. Past influences evident from history are drawn on in order to trace the use of clandestine graves in Australia. Lost bodies or graves show as points of interest. The lonely burial in scrubland has a strong presence in the cultural history of Australia, including the iconographic image of the lost child in the Australian bush. An example is the graves of Burke and Wills (explorers in Australia's early days of settlement) and the search for their bodies. It is resonant of the feelings attached to the idea of a body being 'lost' in an unknown location. The clandestine grave is indeed representative of a lonely grave, unmarked and untended.

Professional Search Bodies

The general public knows relatively little about clandestine graves. Usually, press releases only record that a body has been discovered in a clandestine grave, or simply 'found'. It is often an accidental find. Other times it is the result of difficult searches undertaken by professionals. The families of murder victims whose bodies lie in shallow, lonely, unknown graves are grateful for their efforts, as they are able to bring their bodies to a resting place closer to home.

As the need for expertise has increased (and murder victims continue to be disposed of in this way), multidisciplinary professional bodies have been formed to assist police in the search process. Examples are Necrosearch International, based in Colorado, and the Forensic Search Advisory Group, based in the United Kingdom. Related activities include those of the University of Tennessee's Anthropological Research Facility (or 'body farm') and more recently the Texas State University's Forensic Anthropology Centre, that are established to research aspects of human decomposition. The Argentine Forensic Anthropology Team (EAAF) direct their efforts towards victims of political upheavals and the unorthodox burials of political victims. The Federal Bureau of Investigation (FBI) in Virginia formed the Technology Assisted Search Team (TAST) in 1995 for the purpose of technology-aided evidence retrieval, including the detection of shallow buried bodies (Freeland et al., 2003). Other organisations, such as ERA Technology (based in the United Kingdom), provide expertise in the operation of geophysical equipment in order to assist police searches for bodies. Many of these groups assist police on a voluntary or non-profit basis.

My purpose in writing this book has been to produce a compendium on the anthropology of clandestine graves and the victims within. It is a subject that has largely been ignored and, in book form, is designed to provide a compact reference for those who find themselves called on to search for missing persons who have met a tragic fate. Other readers will find a greater understanding of the science and culture that lies behind clandestine graves, so often a key component of both real life and fiction. It is not the last statement on the subject and indeed warrants continued interest and research. These bodies deserve to be found, and deserve more than the anonymous disposal that is accorded to them. Although it becomes apparent early in the book that there is no instant subsurface X-ray search machine, it is revealed that there are techniques that increase the likelihood of success with professional patience, persistence and a knowledge-based approach.

2

Locating Burial Victims Through Science

In the late 20th century, searching for clandestine graves emerged as a specialised field, concurrent with the development of the wider field of forensic sciences. From being an area solely tackled by police, it became a subject of exploration primarily for anthropologists and archaeologists, but it also involved other specialists. The location of buried bodies as a practice has been developed from within the disciplines of anthropology, archaeology and geophysics, and has relied on significant contributions from the disciplines of botany, entomology and soil science. Although the simple ground search by investigators is still the starting point in any search, a range of other tools and information from research studies now significantly enhances the likelihood of locating buried murder victims. This chapter traces the development of a scientific approach to the location of graves and describes the range of techniques that have been explored to find buried bodies.

Clandestine graves are found in two ways: accidentally or through an investigation. How does one begin to find a buried body? This has been the responsibility of police services since the system of policing was introduced in industrialised societies during the 19th century. Locating a clandestine grave within the context of an investigation is therefore very different from an archaeological search for a historical burial. In the archaeological dig, not only are family members of the deceased also long dead, but time limits are less pressured (usually being largely determined by available funding) and the potential location of the excavation site is usually sourced through historical documentation or associated land features.

The forensic search for a burial, in contrast, is driven by police investigators and is prompted by a search for a missing person who is suspected to have been murdered. When a person is missing, there is an imperative to find the person as quickly as possible to resolve the case, and to relieve the angst of the family and friends of the victim. Once an area is targeted for information gathering, police search for graves by 'surface observation' is the first stage of all such searches. This ground search requires walking over the suspected area of burial and is often called an 'emu search' in Australia, because it mimics the way those large birds closely watch the ground as they strut. For most people, searching for a clandestine grave will be associated with images of police officers in a straggling line with eyes to the ground, walking slowly over an area of scrubland. Some searches result in many hours of hard labour, digging over a large area where information has led police to target their expectations. It is a simple and less costly form of investigation but has limitations, such as personnel not knowing key indicative signs of clandestine graves. Dogs trained in scent detection are often incorporated by police into searches (either trained to respond to cadaver scents or the specific scent of an individual).

When time and resource-consuming searches did not locate murder victims, police began to draw on external sources of help, notably since the 1970s and increasing in the 1980s. Accordingly, scientific principles began to be applied by archaeologists, police officers (Imaizumi, 1974; Boyd, 1979; Hoving, 1986), geophysical experts (Nobes, 2000), anthropologists (France et al., 1992; Owsley, 1995) and psychologists.

During this early engagement phase in the late 20th century, experienced anthropologists and archaeologists, confronted with the difficulties encountered in locating buried human remains, found there was no scientific or proven method to draw on (e.g., Schwartz, 1993; Wright, 1996). Source material about locating graves was scarce or nonexistent, as the greater proportion of literature on forensic searches assumed the body had been found or described the body recovery process itself (McLaughlin, 1974; Skinner & Lazenby, 1993). At the time, scientific principles had not been diligently applied to the search for graves, but rather to the excavation process itself. We can see that the subject of locating buried human remains slowly began to be included from the 1980s, albeit briefly, in broader archaeological, taphonomic, anthropological and then forensic reference books (Krogman & Iscan, 1986; Killam, 1990; Chamberlain, 1994; Hunter, Roberts, & Martin, 1996; Dirkmaat & Adovasio, 1997; Pickering & Bachman, 1997; Lindemann, 2000; Davenport, 2001; Byers, 2002).

The experts engaged by police were faced with the pragmatism of the crime scene scenario; the opportunity for preparation was often limited and the chain of evidence must be preserved during any investigative work. With no solid research base from which to draw, anthropologists and others undertook searches for buried human remains largely on a case-by-case basis; that is, trying techniques in actual investigations rather than techniques based on source studies.

The attempts to approach the location of buried human remains using a scientific basis in this period sit within the context of the growing area of forensic science. Forensic science emerged during the 1980s and 1990s as a discipline with a specific niche that separated it from science as the broader field. Forensic science was no longer confined to the presentation of evidence in court, but could be extended to the investigation process. In practical terms, this is not new; there are accounts of the long history of forensic endeavours prior to the term 'forensic' being in use to resolve legal issues (e.g., Pickering & Bachman, 1997, give a history of forensic anthropology that is traced to the American civil war). Forensic anthropology from the 1980s, in particular, experienced considerable change and was being used by most areas of the judiciary from law enforcement, the coroners, and medical examiners. With respect to clandestine graves, anthropologists' skills in detecting disturbed areas where holes or graves were dug were recognised in terms of the time and expense this could save in recovering buried remains (Reichs, 1992).

In this context, psychologists concentrated on developing the 'profiles' (or typologies) of persons committing particular types of crime as a way of predicting behaviour during and after the crime. Geographic profiling is a field of psychology that aims to associate locales with a perpetrator based on patterns of behaviour. This technique tends to be linked to an individual and is more useful in serial murders, because there is more spatial information. This area is not addressed in this book, as it is sufficiently covered elsewhere and rests largely on there being more than one burial by an individual.

From the 1970s, approaches to locating graves or identifying distinguishing features of graves that might lead to their location have explored three main avenues: identifying surface differences between the grave and its surrounds, identifying differences between the grave and its surrounds that emanate from the grave itself (such as chemical differences within the soil), and identifying differences within the subsurface that may be detected using instrumentation applied from the surface (geophysical instruments). Controlled studies that were able to produce documented observable surface traits of a grave began in the 1980s.

One of the earliest published examples of scientific principles being applied to an actual search for buried human remains is by a Japanese police officer. Imaizumi (1974) successfully located a body during a prolonged search in Japan using a modified soil probe. A litmus test for alkalinity was incorporated into the soil probe, based on the theory that decomposition of the body would produce a high percentage of alkaline substances that could be confirmed in the field. Testing for alkalinity using a soil probe is the only subsurface detection instrument that has been specifically modified to detect properties associated with the body itself and its interactions with the burial environment. This successful location demonstrated the potential to consider the burial in terms of an identifiable difference within its context.

Other ways in which attempts were made to locate graves from the 1980s were broad ranging and explorative, as experts sought to identify a human body below the ground surface using non-invasive methods. The next part of the chapter describes these varied methods, several being the subject of ongoing research and others experimented with briefly.

Use of Dogs

Dogs have been an integral part of searches for missing persons, either alive or buried. These specially trained dogs may be called scent or cadaver dogs depending on the basis of their training. For example, some dogs may be trained to scent decomposing flesh and others to signal at the presence of a human trail. There have been many success stories of dogs locating missing persons, but it is also true that scent dogs are not an infallible method of location. Variation in training techniques, our relatively poor understanding of the dogs' capacity to scent and variation across canine breeds, combined with the fact that dogs are living beings that have daily varying capacities (they may not be well, they tire, and respond to changing temperatures and wind velocities), contribute to this potential for missing a clandestine grave. The substances on which dogs are trained might vary according to the trainer and the availability of real or simulated scents (whether from decaying animal meat, synthetic decomposed material or fresh meat).

Aerial Surveillance

Aerial surveillance is a means of scanning large distances in short periods of time, especially in situations where the area of possible burial is large. Certainly, aerial photography has been used for archaeological site discovery from the early part of the 20th century (McManamon, 1984; Chamberlain, 1994). For example, aerial surveillance was used as part of a strategy to locate a historic mass grave a century-and-a-half-old in north-west Ireland (Ruffell, McCabe, Donnelly, & Sloan, 2009). In that situation, aerial photography records from the 1950s were able to be accessed, which enabled the targeting of likely sites through the identification of mature trees, existing or buried features to be plotted and the topography to be analysed. After a likely site was marked out, geophysical surveys were carried out.

The effectiveness of aerial surveillance is increased if there are comparative photographs available of the targeted areas taken before the alleged burial. The photographs must be taken from a suitably low height. In some countries, such as the United Kingdom, landscapes are photographed regularly by air for mapping purposes, which provides a database of possible source photographs for comparative purposes.

Although aerial surveillance is often used to locate potential mass graves, there seem to be no available accounts where a hidden body has been successfully located in a forensic search. In practice, single graves are too small, with features that do not provide enough contrast from flying heights for this method to be effective (Chamberlain, 1994). At the grave research site described in Chapter 6, for example, aerial surveillance did not find any traces of six animal graves in Australian scrubland that had been markedly disturbed by foxes (Powell, 2006).

Thermal Imaging

Infrared photography, sometimes from aircraft, has been applied to the detection of gravesites. This technique might potentially detect a buried body, because decaying material radiates heat differently to nondecaying material (Davenport, 2001). Variations could be from many other sources, besides a buried body, and the region's capacity to retain heat in the upper soil layers must be considered in terms of the degree of temperature difference that could be expected to appear on the photographs (Duncan, 1983).

The limited research undertaken on this method shows highly variable results. For example, McLaughlin (1974) reported that infrared photography did not detect bodies buried at approximately 1–1.5 m deep in a state of rapid decomposition, but yet detected a grave 48 hours after burial. In contrast, a two-week-old grave was not detected.

This technique has not been the subject of other research on clandestine graves and might be more suited to larger objects. Okamato, Yoshi, Chunliang, Hirotsugu, & Inagaki (1997) applied the thermal image method using an infrared radiometer to verify the position of buried tombs. The results showed an abnormal temperature distribution of the surface over the buried objects, but the target objects were considerably larger than a single set of buried bones.

Chemical Traces of Clandestine Graves

The chemical traces of a buried body within the ground have been considered and explored in the search for clandestine graves. Owsley (1995) commented that higher concentrations of potassium, copper and especially manganese in soils surrounding a decomposing body can be identified through chemical analysis. The more common focus is on the estimation of time since death and decomposition rather than long-term experiments on bone geochemistry or burials by physical anthropologists (Radosevich, 1993). Archaeological studies point to the potential for detecting the presence of buried human remains through elements remaining in the burial environments. There is an interesting history of phosphate testing for archaeological site discovery, such as tests for various phosphorous compounds that are stable and relatively widespread in archaeological features and anthropic soil horizons (McManamon, 1984). For example, Keeley, Hudson, and Evans (1977) found higher concentrations of phosphorous, manganese and copper in body silhouettes of archaeological graves in Mucking, Essex, compared with the surrounding soil. Phosphorous levels were high in places where the bones had survived rather than deteriorated.

Human bodies contain a considerable amount of phosphorous (Chamberlain, 1994) and it has been stated that decomposition of human bodies results in an 'enrichment of phosphate levels in the vicinity of the inhumation' (Chamberlain, 1994, p. 48). As phosphorous remains in the soil for long periods and is not leached from the soil like other elements (such as carbon, nitrogen or calcium), phosphorous has the potential to be used in some way as a detector of buried human remains. Chamberlain (1994) cites the higher levels of phosphorous up to 10 cm below burials in Yorkshire, although these returned to background levels at greater depths. Notably, Rodriguez and Bass (1985) found that soil alkalinity increased just above and just below shallow-buried cadavers during a 12-month period.

Soil type and conditions will impact on trace elements remaining in the soil at a detectable level in comparison with the surrounds (Henderson, 1987; Chamberlain & Pearson, 2001). The effect of added fertilizers, although these are generally applied only to surface layers of soil, must be taken into consideration in most burial circumstances (Chamberlain, 1994).

By obtaining a greater understanding of the chemistry associated with human decay processes, this information may be used to enhance or develop methods to locate clandestine burials. Vass, Bass, Wolt, Foss, & Ammons (1992) carried out a study on time since death using soil solution. Seven cadavers were placed on soil surfaces (not buried) during decomposition. They found distinct patterns for volatile fatty acids (extracted between soil particles) in the soil solution during decomposition and for specific anions and cations (negatively and positively charged ions, respectively) once all that remained were the skeletons. In their preliminary studies, they found that sulphate remained present in large amounts after 4 years (1992). Further, calcium continued to show a cyclic release from skeletal material that was found in substantial quantities. This research relates to bodies above ground and it is not known how durable these findings are in a burial situation.

Later, Vass et al. (2008) carried out experiments to identify the chemical compounds able to be detected at the grave surface as a result of human decomposition. The purpose was to define the odour of decomposition of human remains detectable from the surface of shallow graves. The experiments involved the burial at 0.46–1.07 m of four human bodies over four years. The research of Vass et al. has identified 30 compounds labelled key markers of human decomposition detected at the soil surface. These compounds were produced below the decomposing body and migrated towards the surface through the soil column. Although these key marker compounds are not unique to the human body, being found in background soil samples, it is the elevated level and concentration below and above the corpses in comparison with the controls that is critical.

In other explorations of chemical signatures within gravesoils, Carter and Tibbett (2008) identified a high release of ninhydrin reactive nitrogen (NRN) in the gravesoil of rats buried for 28 days. This experiment was premised on the release of a form of nitrogen into the surrounding burial environment during decomposition. The NRN released in this short post-burial time was twice that of the control soils.

The body emits gases as it decomposes. This feature has been considered for the purposes of detecting buried human remains. McLaughlin (1974) used Vapor-Tect equipment (for the detection of methane, hydrogen phosphide, carbon dioxide, ammonia, hydrogen and hydrogen sulphide 'rotten egg' gases) to verify the presence of a body buried for up to 10 years. To detect gases, the instrument must be close enough to the body to test for any vapours released, which limits this method's usefulness to the confirmation of a buried body in a search area rather than the location of potential burial sites. There is, however, continued exploration into detecting odours from decomposing bodies (e.g., at the University of Tennessee's Anthropological Research Facility).

Scanning of the Subsurface

As yet, search equipment is not purpose designed for crime scene or forensic work (Thomas, 1999), but identifying features below the ground surface has been an activity of archaeologists and geologists, among others, for some time. It is from these areas that geophysical instruments were seen as having the potential to detect clandestine graves. Geophysical instruments have been used extensively in archaeology since the 1950s (McManamon, 1984; Pendick, 1998, Scollar, Tabbagh, Hesse, & Herzog, 1990), including being applied by archaeologists to unmarked cemetery graves. Although geophysical remote sensing instruments have been applied in these and other associated commercial situations, such as for locating pipelines or cables, or ordinance devices (that are all relatively small objects), detecting buried human remains has yielded less predictable results.

The many studies on the detection of cemetery burials using geophysical instruments dating more particularly from the 1990s show the highly variable survey results from burials that would be expected to have more pronounced anomalous subsurface characteristics compared with a shallow-buried set of remains. They also set the context in which geophysical instruments came to be seen as a convenient solution to detecting buried human remains. Several key studies are included here.

Bevan (1991) carried out nine geophysical surveys over historical burial sites and cemeteries in the United States, using the ground penetrating radar (GPR) and electromagnetic (EM) induction. The results had mixed success, with the GPR providing results that suggested graves where there were none and not detecting known graves. Graves in which bones had been reburied were not detected by GPR.

Bevan (1991) also used a Geonics EM38 EM induction meter at a 19th-century Shaker cemetery in Kettering, Ohio. Six of the almost 30 anomalies (defined as low or negative values of apparent conductivity compared with surrounding high values) were selected for shallow excavations. Five graves were identified at a depth of less than 1 m.

Davis et al. (2000) used GPR in 1998 to locate the graves of seven men who died in 1918 and were buried in a cemetery in Norway. The GPR detected voids in uncollapsed coffins, but where the coffins had collapsed there was little contrast in the electrical properties of the materials. They concluded that electrically conductive soils, such as clay, attenuate the GPR signal, thereby severely limiting any possibility of detecting collapsed coffins and bones.

Nobes (1999) applied an EM survey, magnetometer-gradiometer and GPR in combination to survey Maori graves in a New Zealand cemetery. Although he could not excavate and confirm his survey results, he found various anomalous responses. In Australian cemeteries, GPR has been successfully used to detect Aboriginal graves buried in European style after colonisation (L'Oste-Brown, Goodwin, & Yelf, 1996; Long & von Strokirch, 2003).

Buck (2003) carried out geophysical surveys of several cemeteries in the USA. The bodies were buried approximately 2 m deep in metal coffins and surveys were carried out using GPR and a caesium magnetometer (MAG). In sandy clay loam covering volcanic sediment, the tests gave negative results and did not detect known gravesites. At Fort Hood, Texas, GPR and electrical resistivity were used on a small family cemetery (the soil type was coarse sandy gravel). The GPR survey contained some ambiguous anomalies, but not enough to reach confident conclusions. At another cemetery of silty loam soil type, although no potential anomalies were detected by the GPR, excavation revealed grave features. The caesium MAG was also tested on a trench, backfilled only a few days before (2.5 m deep, 1.5 m wide in silty clay loam). Neither the GPR nor the MAG detected the trench.

Cemetery graves have a greater range of distinctive features than do the simple burial of a body within a shallow dug hole. Even where bodies are buried in coffins that provide larger surface areas and reflector surfaces for detection by GPR, geophysical remote sensing survey results are ambiguous or do not provide sufficient information to lead to the reliable detection of gravesites. Despite the inconsistency of results, their application has continued to be explored in forensic searches.

Mellett (1992) used GPR to locate the body of a missing person in a forensic case at a depth of 0.5 m. Although metal objects resulted in a reflection, the humerus (upper arm bone) reflection was also shown. He contended that bone continues to leach calcium into the surrounding soil after interment. The calcium salts are posited as making the bone and the immediate surrounding area more electrically conductive, rendering it visible to radar pulses.

Nobes (2000) applied both GPR and EM surveying to search for a body buried (without a coffin) for almost 12 years in a plantation forest in New Zealand. The body was successfully located through an isolated EM anomaly that was found to be coincident with the body rather than being located with the GPR. The body had allegedly been buried initially in a shallow grave and later transferred to a deeper grave, approximately 1.2 m deep, and tree harvesting and tree stump removal had taken place in the area.

Davenport (2001) describes a case in which GPR was used, where anomalies under a concrete slab were given priority for excavation, revealing human remains.

There have been differing views expressed regarding the effectiveness of geophysical instruments in detecting buried human remains. Chamberlain (1994) asserts that 'conventional geophysical survey methods', such as magnetometry and resistivity, are not useful for locating single burials. This is particularly the case in urban areas where 'secondary disturbances' may result in complicated signals distorting the survey reading. While I was at the Federal Bureau of Investigation Evidence Response Unit in Quantico, a member of the technical team agreed with the experience of high variation in test results using GPR. For example, during a test run, the GPR survey readings showed two clearly defined hyperboles and a third that was barely discernible. It was in this third that a coffin was buried.

There are relatively few controlled studies on the capacity of geophysical instruments to detect decomposing animals or cadavers. Of these studies, GPR is the most commonly applied instrument. The published controlled studies involve either the burial of pigs (France et al., 1992; France et al., 1997; Schultz, Falsetti, Collins, Koppenjan, & Warren, 2002) or human cadavers (Freeland, Miller, Yoder, & Koppenjan, 2003) for the purpose of systematically testing the veracity of geophysical instruments. Schultz et al. (2002) buried pigs and applied GPR over a 21-month period, and Freeland et al. tested GPR on decomposing shallow-buried human cadavers over a 5-month period after burial (these studies are discussed in more detail later).

Schultz et al. (2002) showed that soil type was an influencing factor in burial detection by GPR. The discernment of skeletal pig remains by GPR was compared with that of decomposing pigs. The team carried out GPR surveys over 24 pig burials for 21 months in Florida at two burial depths: approximately 0.5 m and 1 m. It was found that in clay, grave anomalies were more difficult to detect over time, despite there being little decomposition. The pig cadaver survey results were faint, but the grave shaft was discerned. In contrast, those pigs buried in sandy soil were detected throughout the 21-month period. Anomaly characteristics pertaining to the grave in sand are stated as comprising the disturbed soil, the outline of the interface between disturbed soil and undisturbed soil and the body. In sand, these characteristics were the same if the pig was skeletonised or not. Comparison with control graves (not containing a pig) demonstrated that over time, the reflection from the disturbed soil decreased until it was finally no longer detected in sand. In contrast, a skeletonised pig buried for 19 months showed reflections from both the grave wall and the skeleton. This study suggests that after a time period, graveshafts may not be detected due to the resettling of soil.

In a later study, Schultz, Collins and Falsetti (2006) found that GPR can detect pig cadavers in sand (in Florida) at shallow depths when in advanced stages of decomposition and skeletonised (up to 21 months postburial). For pig cadavers buried close to a clay horizon, although soil disturbances were still discernible, it was increasingly difficult to detect the non-skeletonised pig carcass after 12 months.

Freeland et al. (2003) used two GPR instruments to survey control shallow graves containing unembalmed fleshed human cadavers, buried at a depth of 0.6 m at the University of Tennessee's Anthropological Research Facility. The decomposing cadavers were buried alongside artifacts, such as construction debris, metal, wood stones in soil comprising red clay in the subsoil and silt loam in surface. A folded plastic tarp covered the lower half of the body and a 1-metre thick concrete slab covered the gravesite. It is stated that the decomposing body mass within the torso was identified by the GPR, and also the grave walls and folded tarp covering the lower body.

Miller (2002) buried eight decomposing or near skeletal remains beneath concrete slabs in a series of six plots ranging in depth from 0.3 to 1.8 m. The graves were surveyed over a period of nine months at monthly intervals using GPR. Miller found that eight months after burial, the margins of the burial trenches could be detected. More extreme conditions of either heat or cold were considered not conducive to obtaining good survey data.

Pringle, Jervis, Cassella, & Cassidy (2008) carried out geophysical surveys using several different instruments over a 3-month period at a clandestine grave in the United Kingdom in a highly disturbed area constructed to simulate a forensic scene containing a synthetic skeleton and animal organ material. The geophysical instruments applied were bulk ground resistivity, self-potential survey, bulk ground conductivity surveys, magnetic fluxgate gradiometry, magnetic susceptibility survey, electrical resistivity surveys and GPR. It was found that the electrical resistivity survey was the most successful at resolving the grave and recommended surveying after three months. GPR survey results identified subtle anomalies and required significant effort in data acquisition, processing and visualisation. The authors recommend the use of bulk ground resistivity surveys combined with GPR surveys for urban (disturbed) environments.

There has been little research on the effectiveness of the combined use of geophysical instruments; for example, in what order and how to apply combined methods in different soil types, particularly to rule out there being a body within a given area. The study by France et al. (1992; 1997) was the only controlled experiment for some time to have tested more than one type of instrument. In detecting the graves of shallow-buried pigs, France et al. (1997) reported the most useful instruments to be the MAG, EM profiling and GPR. In this study, emphasis is placed on the instruments' capacity to detect subsurface anomalies rather than the body itself. They state the MAG surveys detect areas of excavation, which is attributed to a reorientation of magnetic soil particles after backfilling the graves. Electromagnetic surveys were considered more useful than MAG surveys, because of the influence on ground conductivity from the increased porosity of the backfill materials. However, these studies omit useful pieces of information, such as the percentage and number of gravesites detected and whether the calibration sites were detected, being disturbed ground. The conclusion from the studies was that GPR was the most useful instrument for this purpose due to its capacity to detect soil changes and excavation patterns.

For magnetic surveys to be successful, it is preferable there be a well-formed soil with magnetic properties. Decomposition of the buried body can result in magnetic enhancement through the activity of bacterial activity, but such potential signals are likely to be fairly weak and not easily detected.

The use of geophysical instruments in archaeological practice and their application to cemetery graves and mass grave searches has led to an overexpectation of their capacity in the search for a single clandestine grave. In the forensic search situation, the potential anomalies within the landscape are significantly reduced in scale and highly dependent on surrounding conditions. When a survey reading is not produced, this does not necessarily mean a body is not present, especially in a grave that has existed for several years.

The Surface of the Clandestine Grave

One of the earliest landmark studies published on buried human remains was from Rodriguez and Bass (1985), who carried out controlled burials of unembalmed human cadavers buried in shallow trenches (0.3–1.2 m deep) from one month up to one year. This was pioneering work in which they made observations on plant growth, soil resettling and soil coloration, all visible from the surface.

Further work on the grave surface was not published until the following decade. France et al. (1992, 1997) studied pig burials over a five-year period. This is a significant contribution, because the research team discussed 'multidisciplinary methods' of gravesite location, which included observing surface changes and testing several geophysical instruments over the gravesites. They recognised the potential of other disciplines to contribute to gravesite location, such as botany, geology and geophysics. This study raised the issue of the surface recovery of gravesites, noting that climatic conditions are important to gravesite recovery and plant establishment, the key element being moisture (1997).

The study by France et al. (1992) showed that it is possible to identify disturbed ground through vegetation changes, but that different vegetation patterns are not necessarily indicators of the presence of a body within a grave. They found that 'pioneer or opportunistic', plants sometimes called 'weeds' were the first to grow on the gravesites, including plants that were not previously present. The disturbed plots (regardless of the presence of a body) continued to be visually different from the surrounds for five years. Plant diversity had not been specifically addressed until the study by France et al., in which it was found that undisturbed plots or nongrave areas showed a greater diversity of plants compared with disturbed plots, irrespective of whether the graves contained pig remains.

Further, the study by France et al. (1992) showed that although it is a common belief that the additional nutrients provided by a body within a grave will affect plant growth, there was no noticeable difference between the calibration pits (burial pits that did not contain pigs) and those containing pigs after five years of burial (1997). It was concluded that disturbance of the soil was the key variable, and not the body, as a source of nutrients. This same research team later became known as Necrosearch International, a voluntary group of professionals who assist police in body locations in the United States.

Soil characteristics were also a source of noticeable difference between a grave and its surrounds. For example, Owsley (1985) also commented on the different coloured (excess) soil that could be found near the grave as a result of digging the grave. Comparative soil compaction was identified by anthropologists as a potential indicator of a burial and could be measured via the use of the soil probe, as it detects variations in the density of the subsurface. Owsley (1995) effectively used the soil probe in two forensic cases that resulted in the successful location of buried bodies.

It was quickly recognised that the clandestine grave would serve as an attractant for fauna. Signs of faunal activity were identified as surface indications of a potential gravesite, because of the inherent source of food to some animals (Galloway et al., 1989; Janaway, 1996; Haglund, 1997; Murad, 1997; France et al., 1997). These signs included scattered bones at the ground surface at varying distances from the gravesite, or signs of burrowing to reach the buried body. In Australia, research has shown that scavenging at clandestine graves can continue for some years after burial (Powell, 2006). Figure 2.1 shows an example of animal scavenging in South Australia. A human mandible was dragged a short distance from a hidden body.

Specific plant growth at the gravesite has received very limited attention, although Carter and Tibbett (2003) explored field mycology as a potential means of locating and recovering buried human remains. They considered particular chemoecological groups of fungi (ammonia fungi and postputrefaction fungi) as surface grave indicators. Fungi and bacteria are known to be the major organisms decomposing dead leaves and other organic matter. Although organic matter is broken down, it is also transformed into fungi and bacteria as these organisms feed on the organic matter and reproduce.

FIGURE 2.1
Human mandible removed by animals.
Source: SA Police, published with permission.

Carter and Tibbett make the observation that ammonia and postputrefaction fungi types fruit when nitrogen is released after burial following decomposition of the cadaver. This implies some connection between the fruiting and the amount of nitrogen released from a cadaver.

The engagement by police of other professions noted for their expertise in locating buried objects (such as anthropologists, archaeologists, geologists and geophysical experts) provided the impetus for research. A gap in knowledge in the growing area of forensic science was highlighted in this way. The clandestine grave became the focus of several research and field studies, although ongoing research has been limited. To date there has been little critical analysis and too few studies about locating buried human remains, most especially regarding the application of geophysical instruments. Although the presence of anomalies may be detected by geophysical instruments, the presence of a body is not able to be definitively ascertained (Bevan, 1991; Nobes, 2000; Davenport, 2001). Conversely, not obtaining any results from geophysical surveys at this stage cannot be used to state categorically that a body is not buried in an area. In a search situation it is valuable to be able to state categorically that there is no body buried in an area.

3

Grave Surfaces

It was only a depression in the ground, the kind that might have been made, years past, by the falling of one of the great stones. Or by a grave . . .

Mary Stewart, *The Crystal Cave* (1970)

Graves are artifacts and do not occur as natural phenomena. In simple physical terms, a burial is an interference with a landscape; an inhumation of a new and foreign object into an environment (either natural or developed). A burial critically disrupts and alters that ecosystem in content and form, and subsequently itself becomes subject to the same environmental conditions as its surrounds. This chapter describes the clandestine grave in terms of its physical impact on the landscape and the changes as they appear from the surface.

It was difficult for early investigators to know what a clandestine grave might look like in different environments, especially if a significant amount of time had passed since the suspected burial. A search for the image of the telltale burial mound of starkly contrasting soil to the surrounding area may be unrealistic for several reasons; the murderer is unlikely to have left a mound of dirt, weathering will impact on the surface appearance, and vegetation may have grown around the grave.

To locate a gravesite, we need to examine the surface appearance of a gravesite and consider the likely changes over time. The issues that become important are the degree to which the disturbed area (gravesite) might be affected by weathering processes and environmental conditions compared with its surrounds, whether or not there is a 'catch-up period' when the differences are obfuscated (at least to the naked eye), the duration of the various characteristics of graves after burial and any subsequent characteristics evident later in time that appear anomalous to the wider landscape surface.

When a grave is created, the following changes occur in the landscape:

- an alteration of the upper visible surface area (e.g., displacement and disturbance of vegetation, surface litter or debris);
- soil upheaval and its subsequent settling (disruption of stratigraphic layering within the hole dug, mixing of the soil horizons, followed by soil consolidation and the formation of depressions);
- the deposition of a food source for foragers and insects; and
- the possibility of artefacts left at or within the gravesite (belongings and clothing, tools or weapons).

When the Grave is Created

A grave is created in a regular manner, beginning with a hole dug downwards into the ground from the surface, forming a cavity into which a body will be interred at varying depths. Graves (either ritual burials or clandestine graves) are not constructed on an angle as in a burrow. Surface plant material is uprooted where the hole is begun and upcast soil deposited on top of the adjacent surrounds, damaging any neighbouring plant growth. Soil from below the surface is lifted out, aerated unintentionally and mixed with the different horizons (upcast), altering the stratification of the subsurface soil in that area permanently (Dirkmaat and Adovasio, 1997; Pickering and Bachman, 1997). The body is placed within the grave and the pile of soil that was been removed from the ground is returned to the hole, to cover the body and refill the grave.

The size of the grave will depend on the instruments used to dig the grave (shovels, picks, crowbars or backhoes), the strength of the person or persons digging, time available, and most importantly, the soil type and underlying terrain. For reasons of expediency, and the difficulties associated with digging a grave, victims of murder tend to be buried in relatively shallow graves. The grave may be dug in a rectangular fashion or dipping oval cavity, but will largely be dictated by the hardship of digging into the subsurface that may have embedded rocks or tree roots. The shape of a grave will usually be that of an oval or oblong and will not have irregular narrow extended areas, for example, in which an upstretched arm is placed or spreadeagled legs. Relaying the upcast soil over the grave will give the gravesite surface an oval appearance initially.

The digging of a grave results in an area of upheaval around the grave, which will correspond to the size of the grave; the larger or deeper the grave, the greater is the surrounding area that is changed (Hunter, 1997).

Even a small grave will produce a larger disturbed surface area than the actual diameter of the grave. Digging a grave removes not only the surface growth, but also what may be classified as natural 'debris or organic litter'. This debris comprises a layer of dry leaves, pods, gumnuts, dead flowers, twigs and branches that have dropped from trees or other plants, or have been wind blown to settle on the ground surface. The debris settles and compacts over time, accumulating and mounting unless removed in some way. If removed, it cannot be replaced in the same way, because it would have been aerated. Upcast over the grave is clearly visible without this surface layer of debris. The continued visibility of the upcast is an important aspect to the location of graves and will be impacted by the deposition of surface debris and subsequent vegetation growth.

Figure 3.1 shows the difference between the soil layering in undisturbed soil and that of the clandestine grave. Undisturbed soil has distinct soil horizons, that is, layers of soil formations. The only likely exceptions are soil types with no soil horizons at the shallow depths associated with most forensic burials, such as sand and desert environments, sites of landfill or areas that have already had the soil horizons mixed. The soil that is lifted out of the ground has been termed 'upcast'. 'Backfill' is the term that has been given to earth returned into the grave (Hunter & Martin, 1996). I use the single term 'upcast' throughout, because I am referring to the same soil; the upcast or soil that is dug up from the gravesite and returned to the same area. Any excess upcast spread around the area will cause further damage to the surrounding vegetation (Duncan, 1983).

Subsurface soil is usually of a different colour (lighter or darker) and texture (e.g., it may contain rubble or have a higher clay content) to that on the uppermost surface (Rodriguez & Bass, 1985; Owsley, 1995). This is the common experience of anyone who has tried their hand at gardening, and is due to the underlying stratigraphy of the soil.

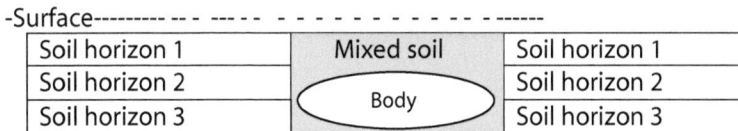

-Surface--------- --- --- -- - - - - - - - - - - -- - ------

Soil horizon 1	Mixed soil	Soil horizon 1
Soil horizon 2	Body	Soil horizon 2
Soil horizon 3		Soil horizon 3

FIGURE 3.1
Soil structure within graves compared to undisturbed surrounds. The line at the top of the figure represents the broken continuity of surface features. Note the soil horizons will vary in depth across different areas.

The way in which a body is placed within the grave will depend on the size of the grave and state of the body. For example, it may be flexed or laid out (or supine). If a body is buried after the onset of rigor mortis, this may impact the degree of difficulty experienced in transporting the body (such as placing it within a vehicle) and the shape and size of the burial pit. In this case, the body is more likely to be buried in an extended position, meaning the burial pit would be the length of the body as compared with if the body was buried in a curled or flexed position. Rigor mortis begins within 2–6 hours after death. Essentially, it is a stiffening of the muscles caused by the disappearance of adenosine triphosphate, which facilitates the contraction of muscles. Adenosine triphosphate is absent approximately 4 hours after death. The process varies with temperature; in hot conditions rigor mortis will begin and end more quickly and in colder conditions it will commence quickly and end slowly (Quigley, 1963). It is complete within 12 hours of death and then it begins to subside (between 12 and 48 hours).

When a body is buried in soil, there may be an excess of soil at the surface level. In a formal burial, an extra mound of soil is placed over the grave to compensate for the resettling of soil. It may be assumed that in a murder case it would be unwise to leave a mound above the grave, even to compensate for any expected soil consolidation (Geberth, 1983), for the simple reason that the intent is to disguise its existence. Actual cases in the literature have not reported mounds as indicators of clandestine graves, although it is possible that mounds over the graves resettle before discovery. It may be assumed that traces of subsurface soil (upcast) will remain around the gravesite after burial, unless the upcast is laid on plastic or a groundsheet. Further, there will be an absence of vegetation on the burial area (unless deliberate replanting has occurred).

Postburial Grave Appearance

In considering the postburial changes to the landscape, we are accounting for the resilience of the site at which a body has been buried. What is the capacity of the ground surface to absorb the changes introduced and recover to resemble its original appearance? Figure 3.2 shows an actual site at which a body was located, from police files. It was taken after the victim's body was recovered. Although it is a recovery rather than a burial, some insight is given as to how a landscape is changed after a hole is dug of this size.

After the body is buried, the gravesite will be subject to weathering and external conditions. The variables affecting the surface appearance of gravesites will include the position of the grave in relation to the surface terrain (proximity to trees, bushes, riverbeds, and so on), soil type, nearby vegetation, rainfall and the surface gradient. Wildlife will be a potential source of interference with the gravesite.

There have been few case studies about the physical appearance of forensic graves at regular postburial intervals. There are two key studies that are referred to in this section: those of Rodriguez and Bass (1985) and France et al. (1997). There are other more general references to the physical appearance of graves (Krogman & Iscan, 1986; Killam, 1990; Hunter, Roberts, & Martin, 1996; Dirkmaat & Adovasio, 1997; Pickering & Bachman, 1997; Byers, 2002). More recent observations of grave surface changes over several years at animal and human burials in a dry scrubland based environment are described in Chapter 6.

Climatic conditions will govern the rapidity of new vegetation growth over a gravesite. The type of subsurface soil that is brought to the surface after refilling a grave will affect plant growth in relation to the soil's capacity to retain moisture. The location of the gravesite will also impact on the regrowth of vegetation over the gravesite in terms of shelter (whether the burial is beneath trees) and water catchment potential (e.g., if located in sloping ground). This will continue until a stable plant community is established.

FIGURE 3.2
Site of a body recovery.
Source: SA Police, published with permission.

Ecologists and botanists use the term 'plant succession' or 'successional dynamics' to refer to the way in which plants will propagate and grow within an area after a disturbance of vegetation and/or soil (Rees, Condit, Crawley, Pacala, & Tilman, 2001). Early successional plants tend to show high fecundity, long dispersal, rapid growth in high resourced areas and slower growth in lower resourced areas. Conversely, traits ascribed to late successional are: relatively low fecundity, short dispersal, slow growth and the general ability to survive in low resource areas (Rees et al., 2001). Regardless of plant type, immediately after a burial any plants will be smaller and younger than nearby plants.

The application of plant ecology and botany to forensic investigations has been discussed by Duncan (1983), Rodriguez and Bass (1985), Bock and Norris (1997), and France et al., (1997). Detailed knowledge of the vegetation of an area may be helpful in identifying disturbed sites, such as a grave, because succession in vegetation may be able to be predicted for different regions, with regard to early or late successional plant types. It has been stated that disturbances in vegetation can be identified for long periods, even decades, after a disturbance event (Bock & Norris, 1997). This has not been put to the test with respect to clandestine gravesites and it is possible such gravesites may be too small an area.

Vegetation differentiation over a gravesite has been reported as:

- absent or less dense over a recent gravesite (Bock & Norris, 1997; Owsley, 1995)
- more 'lush' over the grave after one year than in the surrounding area because of the less compact, moister soil (Owsley, 1995) and following the first spring after burial (Bock & Norris, 1997), and because of the release of organic materials from the decomposing body (Rodriguez & Bass, 1985)
- showing a difference in the size and height of plants (Duncan, 1983)
- a noticeably different mix of plants on disturbed areas compared with undisturbed areas (France et al., 1997)
- parched vegetation in dry circumstances, where soil on gravesites does not retain moisture as well as the surrounding soil (Hunter & Martin, 1996).

Rodriguez and Bass (1985) observe that the surface indicators often described as relating to graves were not found uniformly over all gravesites. For example, they observed differential plant growth at only two burials, where shorter growth was recorded on one grave and on the other growth occurred more rapidly. Rodriguez and Bass attributed the increased foliage over shallow burials to the release of organic materials from the decomposing body, particularly after a year or more. They believed deeper burials led to reduced plant growth because of the greater disturbance to the soil. There is little evidence for the affect of depth of burial on vegetation growth on grave surfaces and there have been no later studies on this issue. It is equally likely that the deeper and different soil layers brought to the surface as upcast in a deeper burial would influence vegetation growth. Rodriguez and Bass did not comment on plant diversity specifically, nor any differentiation in plant type from the surrounds.

France et al. (1992, 1997), in a longitudinal study (observation over several years) of pig gravesites, described vegetation changes to the pig graves after a 5-year burial period in Colorado. Eighteen gravesites were established, of which 16 contained buried pigs and two were calibration pits (empty gravesites). The depth of burial is not stated. In terms of vegetation patterns, the results showed that:

- undisturbed plots were found to have a greater diversity of plants compared with disturbed plots, irrespective of whether the graves contained a pig
- 'pioneer or opportunistic' plants were the first to grow on the gravesites, including plants that were not previously present
- no plots attained the preburial plant species mix
- the per cent cover for each grave was similar, but the species mix at each site was different
- disturbed plot vegetation changed according to stages of plant succession (specific changes not given)
- the critical factor to gravesite recovery and the establishment of plants was moisture.

France et al. (1997) observed that although it is a common belief that the additional nutrients provided by a body within a grave will affect plant growth, the observations made of both calibration pits and those containing pigs after five years were not noticeably different. Calibration pits and graves show similar revegetation patterns. From this study, we may extrapolate that identifying disturbed ground through vegetation changes can indicate a grave, but that vegetation changes are not necessarily indicators for the presence of a body. They found that the disturbed area, regardless of the presence of a pig, looks different to the surrounding areas (France et al., 1992).

The level of pH in soil affects vegetation. In alkaline soils, which have a high pH, plant growth tends to be healthier because of the higher levels of nutrients available, whereas in acid soils plant growth is not as healthy, indicated by poor colour and less vigorous growth (Killam, 1990). If a decomposing body affects the pH level in soil, then plant growth would be expected to be influenced accordingly, however, there are no case studies demonstrating more lush and sustained plant growth.

Archaeologists have used changes in vegetation to assist in the location of historical sites, including gravesites. For example, in 1949, Woolley identified graves in Carcemish, North Syria, by examining patterns of weed growth in a field that had been ploughed to a depth of 0.75 m. He correctly identified graveshafts by following the patterns of deep-growing weeds, deducing that at some time in the past the gravel and soil had been broken up by digging, thereby allowing the weed roots to penetrate deeper than would normally be possible. Woolley was able to find areas that were disturbed to a greater depth from plants whose roots grew deep in some areas over others.

We know that upcast soil is readily visible over the gravesite after burial. What happens to the soil over time at a grave? The disturbed soil will begin to settle and will be affected by weather conditions, especially the amount of moisture it receives. It is possible to detect soil upheaval by variation in soil settling within an area, thus pointing to a potential gravesite (Imaizumi, 1974; Duncan, 1983; Schwartz, 1993; Owsley, 1995). Unearthed areas will have less compacted soils. These may be recognised by their grain, degree of cracking when moisture content is low in the area and amount of 'give' when pressure is applied, such as can be felt through the application of a soil probe. Spenneman and Franke (1995) found during exhumations in the Marshall Islands of graves (approximately 1.6 m deep) created between 1946 and 1958, that the soil in the interior of the grave was unconsolidated and uncompressed.

Rodriguez and Bass (1985) directed attention to the enduring characteristics of the upcast or backfill itself, noting colour differentiation from the surface soil. Rodriguez and Bass suggested the traces of upcast 'lessen over time' as a result of weathering (in their study of bodies buried from six months to one year). They found the darker colour of the upcast lessened over the study period of six months to one year. No reason is given, although it may be speculated that it could be due to weathering, exposure and possibly the scattering of the grains.

It is likely that the positioning of the body within the grave will affect the resultant signs of consolidation and the subsequent formation of depressions, although no specific studies have determined depression patterns in clandestine burials. Little is known about the pattern of depressions if a body is flexed. The nature of subsurface bloating in a clandestine grave is unknown. It has been stated that if a body is laid prostrate and horizontal, two depressions will be expected. First, a depression will form as the ground begins to slope inwards towards the centre of the grave (Killam, 1990) and a secondary depression may occur over the abdomen area as this collapses, in a shallow grave (Morse, Duncan, & Stoutamire, 1983), but not necessarily in a deeper grave. This assumes the body is laid in a position likely to produce secondary depressions. Duncan (1983) states the main unknown as being the degree of skeletal collapse of the buried victim. However, it may be argued that the collapse of the skeleton would have less impact on the soil space within a grave than the decomposition of the surrounding tissue (which is mostly water), because the soil would gradually seep into the areas previously occupied by tissue as it decomposes. The skeletal components would occupy the same volume in the soil as before decomposition.

Soil compaction has been described as an indicator of a grave (McLaughlin, 1974; Duncan, 1983; Morse et al., 1983; Rodriguez & Bass, 1985; Killam, 1990; France et al., 1992; Owsley, 1995; Hunter & Martin, 1996). This is particularly noted in regard to the appearance of depressions based on the resettling of backfill (Krogman & Iscan, 1986; Killam, 1990) and/or bodily decomposition (Duncan, 1983; Rodriguez & Bass, 1985; Killam, 1990; Owsley, 1995; Hunter & Martin, 1996; Janaway, 1996). As soil consolidates, if there has been no compensatory soil added (in the form of a mound), one would expect to find a dip or shallow 'depression' at the site of the refilled hole. There has been little controlled research into depressions and their formation over gravesites. 'Compaction' is an incorrect use of the term in geological terms, as compaction generally means the reaction of soil to applied external pressure (such as a tractor). What is meant in terms of clandestine graves is the resettling of soil laid in the grave, after rain or postburial climatic conditions. When backfill is reposited over the body to fill in the grave, the soil horizons and any subsurface stratification are mixed together. This soil has been aerated. Over time, rain or the action of gravity will result in the soil particles coming closer together with fewer air spaces.

As indicated earlier, there may be more than one depression at a gravesite, usually described as primary and secondary depressions, meaning there is an overall depression (primary) and a depression within that, which appears as a further 'scoop' (secondary depression). Duncan (1983) states that different soils have different rates of compaction, resulting in a variation of the depth of depressions over different soils. He states a secondary depression 'will normally be found only over a grave of about 24–30 inches (approximately 0.7 m) in depth'. It is posited that the shallower the grave, the more pronounced the secondary depression and that a depression will form more quickly after rain or the input of moisture. Rodriguez and Bass (1985) report the noticeable resettling of soil within the burial trenches varying in the time taken to form depressions from one week to a few months. They state that deeper burials (1.2 m) resulted in the formation of deeper depressions. Secondary depressions (depressions within a depression) were observed at the 0.6 m and 0.3 m gravesites (shallower gravesites). Hunter and Martin (1996) state that greater depressions would be found in deeper burials compared with shallow burials, because a deeper grave would become more compacted.

The capacity of the upcast to retain moisture in comparison with the surrounding undisturbed surface soil would affect the surface appearance of an area; for example, cracking or splitting of the surface may be found at the junction of the upcast and undisturbed ground, or where the grave edges meet surrounding soil (Duncan, 1983). This observation might be related to the different granular texture of upcast (from the mixed soil horizons), which may respond differently to surface climate conditions. It is not known how long this indicator may endure.

In contrast, France et al. (1997) state that at less than five years after burial, 'excavation boundaries tend to become masked, fill material becomes generally more fine-grained, and the compaction of the fill material to the original surface grade is facilitated' (1997, p. 504), but that these changes did not occur during a dry season. Climate and, in particular, moisture, was found to be a significant influence on the duration of the physical characteristics of graves.

The surface appearance of a clandestine grave can be significantly altered by the foraging of fauna. Signs of digging, indicated by small burrows or tracks, insect activity (eggs, larvae) or droppings can point to the presence of a gravesite as a food source for various types of fauna, both large and small (Rodriguez & Bass, 1985; Owsley, 1995; Hunter & Martin, 1996; France et al., 1997; Haglund, 1997). Factors influencing faunal activity may be climatic conditions, depth of burial, concurrent insect activity (impacting on the rate of skeletonisation) and the access and type of scavengers within the burial area. Predators drawn to the scent of a buried body will vary within each country and therefore the distinguishing traces will vary. For example, there are turkey vultures in Colorado; coyotes, raccoons and foxes in Tennessee; foxes and rats in the United Kingdom; wild dogs, dingoes and wild pigs in parts of Australia and foxes in South Australia to cite a few.

Therefore, the processes of weathering, soil settling and vegetation growth may not proceed in a sequential manner, but may themselves be disturbed, and burrowing may be especially indicative of a gravesite. Faunal invasion of a burial includes insect activity and this is discussed in more detail in the next chapter as part of the decomposition process. At this point, surface insect activity may be expected soon after burial, including the marked presence of blowflies over an area. This is especially the case if the burial is shallow.

A burial is a man-made alteration to a relatively small area that breaks any relative homogeneity of the immediate landscape. A burial is distinguished at the surface level from its context, mainly because of changes imposed on the environment through the act of digging a hole rather than the depositing of a body in the ground. The key surface differences between the burial area and its surrounding landscape are related to contrast in soil (colour, texture, degree of compression), differences in plant growth, and absence of compacted and settled organic debris. Animal foraging and its impact on the grave are also surface indicators.

Of critical importance to the process of surface change are the climatic conditions, as this will affect the soil and vegetation, and clearly there will be considerable variation in different environments. The next chapter discusses the interrelationship between the body and the grave environment.

4

What Lies Beneath:
The Buried Body Within the Grave

Nature does not know extinction; all it knows is transformation.

Wernher von Braun, *American Weekly*, 10 February 1963

There are two parts to a grave: what you can see at the surface and what you cannot see lying beneath. The previous chapter described the changes to the surface of the landscape when a hole is dug into the ground for the purpose of depositing a body. This chapter looks at what happens below the surface when the body within decomposes, differentiating the grave from any other hole in the ground. We may view the grave as an active ecosystem, within which the body undergoes a transformation, prompting an exchange of chemicals at the interface between the body and its environment. The investigators' search for a forensic grave will benefit from an understanding of these processes and the environmental factors that will facilitate or impede decomposition.

The examination of death, decomposition and burial falls within the field of taphonomy (Garland, 1987). The taphonomic behaviour of the body is influenced by factors that relate to the body itself (such as the cause of death or state of the body at death, the time interval between death and burial, the treatment of the body prior to burial) and the characteristics of the burial environment (Garland & Janaway, 1989). Decomposition within the burial environment involves complex interactions between many variables, including soil type (in particular, levels of acidity and alkalinity), moisture levels and humidity (Henderson, 1987).

At the moment of death or in its living state, the human body comprises water, dissolved salts, protein, carbohydrates and lipids or oils and fats, and the bones and teeth constitute the mineralised tissues (these latter comprise 7% of the body; Chamberlain & Pearson, 2001). Almost all (99%) of the mass of the human body is made up of six elements: oxygen, carbon, hydrogen, nitrogen, calcium and phosphorous. Within minutes of death, a human body begins the decomposition process (approximately four minutes is given by Vass et al., 2002). The stages of bodily decomposition are

- **Autolysis.** Immediately after death autolysis commences, initiating the destruction of soft tissues during which the skin swells and blisters (Janaway, 1996). Bodily enzymes promote automatic digestion, breaking down proteins and fats, and the body feeds on itself. Eventually, the body will start to decay (putrefaction) or become preserved (mummified) in response to environmental conditions (and this may include the production of adipocere).

- **Putrefaction.** Putrefaction involves enzyme activity and bacteria feeding on the soft tissues of the body. During putrefaction, bacteria may come from two sources: the body itself, especially the respiratory and alimentary tracts (from when it was alive) and the external environment (Chamberlain & Pearson, 2001). Aerobic microorganisms utilising oxygen, together with the formation of gases, create the environment in which the body will reduce (Janaway, 1987). The gases that are formed and released during decomposition are hydrogen phosphide, hydrogen sulphide, ammonia and carbon dioxide.

- **Transformation of the body components to simpler chemical forms.** The soft bodily tissues (protein, carbohydrate and fat components of the body) are reduced to a fluid. One of these products are short-chain fatty acids (Janaway, 1996; McGregor, Wood, & Brecknell, 1996). Insects are attracted to the resulting smell and their subsequent larvae continue to feed on the body's tissues. Fungi will feed on cadavers and will even dissolve bones and teeth.

- **Skeletonisation (defleshed bones).** Eventually, the body will be reduced to skeletal remains with little or no bodily tissues, except where mummification occurs.

- **Deterioration of the skeleton.** Certain soil conditions will promote the deterioration of skeletal remains and others will promote better preservation. Teeth are the more durable components of the skeletal framework.

Factors That Impact Decomposition

The decomposition process will be mitigated, interrupted, promoted or impaired by a range of factors. Each clandestine grave will vary in terms of soil type, depth of burial, general area (such as scrubland, undisturbed ground or developed area), its positioning in relation to other land features (beneath a log, near trees, in an open area) and the way in which the body is buried (such as use of protective wrapping around the body or clothing). Bodies buried for the same length of time will vary in terms of degree of decomposition when buried in different environments.

Decomposition of the body within a grave will be most affected by the following factors: amount of moisture, temperature, oxygen availability, and access of insects and bacteria to the body. Each of these factors will be dependent on the physical locale of the burial. Climate and the geography (soil composition and chemistry, site slope, surface and subsurface water movement) of the burial place will determine temperatures and moisture levels. Other factors affecting decomposition include: season of burial, presence or absence of bodily wounds, amount of cover to the burial area and duration of interment (Dirkmaat & Adovasio, 1997). Below the surface, within the burial site, the variables important to the geochemical conditions include: soil pH, organic matter content, soil solution fluoride and carbonate concentration, mineralogy, and texture, temperature variations, abundance and distribution of precipitation, local groundwater movement and microbial activity (Pate, Hutton, & Norrish, 1989).

Insects and Bacteria

Soft tissues on a body decay first. This destruction is mainly due to necrophilous (dead flesh-eating) insects and bacteria (Mann, Bass, & Meadows, 1990). Insects consume almost all parts of a dead organism, except the skeleton (Lord & Goff, 1994). Therefore, conditions that inhibit or promote insect activity will have a considerable effect on the extent of the decomposition of a human body (Dirkmaat & Adovasio, 1997; Chamberlain & Pearson, 2001). Temperature, in particular, influences the rate of chemical reactions and the amount of bacteria and insect activity. The optimal temperature for bacteria contributing to decomposition is 37°C (Henderson, 1987; Chamberlain & Pearson, 2001).

The process of decay with the accompanying insect and bacteria activity is increased with heat or humidity, and decreased in the cold (Rodriguez & Bass, 1985; Mant, 1987; Komar, 1998). In cold conditions, chemical reactions are slowed, thereby reducing bacterial activity and the hydrolysis of fats and proteins (Chamberlain & Pearson, 2001). For example, Mant (1987) noted that anaerobic putrefactive organism activity was reduced at temperatures below 21°C. In such circumstances, soft tissues are more likely to be preserved.

Extreme conditions, hot or cold, may lead to mummification and inhibit the rate of decay because the action of microbes and insects is inhibited (Henderson, 1987; Thomas, 1995). In hot conditions, water in the body evaporates quickly, drying out the skin and there is no time for bacteria and insects to feed on the flesh (Henderson, 1987). In dry conditions, soft tissues are more likely to be preserved because tissues dehydrate rapidly, reducing bacterial activity, including when a body has become dehydrated prior to burial (Chamberlain & Pearson, 2001). Hydrolysis is reduced or eliminated.

Endogenous enzymes and microorganisms convert neutral fats to adipocere (Janaway, 1996). Adipocere (water-insoluble material composed of hydroxy fatty acids) is the product of a chemical reaction in which fats react with water and hydrogen in the presence of bacterial enzymes, breaking down into fatty acids and soaps. The formation of adipocere is dependent upon moisture, as fat becomes concentrated with moisture, although warm, dry conditions facilitate the formation of adipocere (Janaway, 1996). The action of anaerobic bacteria leads to the formation of adipocere through the slow hydrolysis of fats in the decomposing human body. Ideal conditions for the transformation of fats into adipocere are when there is a lack of oxygen in cold and humid environments, for example, sodden soil. Adipocere has the capacity to help preserve a body because it is resistant to bacteria. Mant (1987) noted the rapid formation of adipocere on those bodies that were fully clothed within damp soil, which serves to preserve bones (McGregor et al., 1996).

Moisture Levels

The way in which the moisture and water content within the burial affect the rate of decomposition is through the support of aerobic bacteria and the promotion of leaching. Reduced oxygen and concentrations of nutrients or water prevent bacterial growth. In this situation, putrefaction is delayed because aerobic bacteria cannot survive (Chamberlain & Pearson, 2001). Waterlogged burials enhance the preservation of proteins in cartilage, skin, hair and nails (Chamberlain & Pearson, 2001). If a body is completely immersed in water, it may be preserved or completely skeletonised.

Soil Type

Different soil types will impact on the extent and rate of the decomposition of a body. Within the grave, the body is enclosed by soil, which is more aerated than surrounding areas (Janaway, 1987). The body itself, when buried directly in soil, may have a mucous sheath around it, formed from liquefied decomposition products and the fine silt fraction from the soil (Janaway, 1987). Porous, permeable and light soils accelerate decomposition, because they promote a relatively free exchange of oxygen and water from the atmosphere and reductive gases (such as carbon dioxide, hydrogen sulphide, ammonia and methane) from the body (Rentoul & Smith, 1973; Janaway, 1996). Conversely, dense, clay-like soils may actively retard decomposition (Rentoul & Smith, 1973). Bodies decompose more slowly in lime soil and faster in moist clay, clay-loess, dry wood humus and in acidic marsh areas (Krogman & Iscan, 1986). Within humic soils, there are high concentrations of bacteria and other organisms that feed on decaying flesh (Pate, Hutton, & Norrish, 1989). In addition, salts in dry soils may reduce microbial activity in buried bodies, while tanning agents in peat bogs preserve collagen molecules (Chamberlain & Pearson, 2001).

Depth of Burial

Depth of burial influences the amount of oxygen available, which affects the decay of soft tissues (Henderson 1987). The processes of decay on the body are more effectively inhibited in deeper burials (Mant, 1987; Chamberlain & Pearson, 2001). In a shallow grave, the decay of the body is promoted because of the greater interchange between the body and the surface. This in turn allows easier access for insects to the body (Thomas, 1995), aeration of the soil by earthworms and greater fluctuations of temperature (Henderson, 1987). The greater increases in temperature from a body decomposing in a shallow grave compared with bodies buried more deeply enhance insect and bacterial activity (Owsley, 1995). This will change as the body cools over time, affecting the temperature appropriate for the growth of endogenous bacteria (Chamberlain & Pearson, 2001). Mann et al. (1990) have stated that shallow buried bodies (0.3 or 0.6 m) may skeletonise in less than 12 months compared with the several years it may take for bodies buried in deeper graves (0.9 or 1.2 m).

Covering Around the Body

Coverings around a buried body will impact on decomposition, because this inhibits access for insects and exogenous bacteria. For example, the body will take longer to decay if wrapped in plastic compared with exposed body parts (Mann et al., 1990). Mant (1987) found that bodies buried directly in soil, but with clothes (even very few clothes), decomposed more slowly than those in a coffin, even where there was a significant degree of airspace.

Figure 4.1 summarises the decomposition process in diagrammatic form. What happens to the soil around the body as it decomposes? Through the process of decomposition, the immediate surrounds of the burial context are altered in some way. The extent of this difference is not fully known. The colour and content of the surface soil will be affected by the results of decomposition as bodily fluids and chemicals seep into the soil, providing the body is not contained in some way, such as in a garbage bag. The products of decomposition (liquefied proteins and fats) are highly soluble in water and percolate through the soil (Chamberlain & Pearson, 2001). Liquefied body products can become fixed onto mineral complexes, which are washed down by groundwater. It has been suggested these are able to be detected as chemical residues 'after thousands of years' (Garland & Janaway, 1989, p. 27).

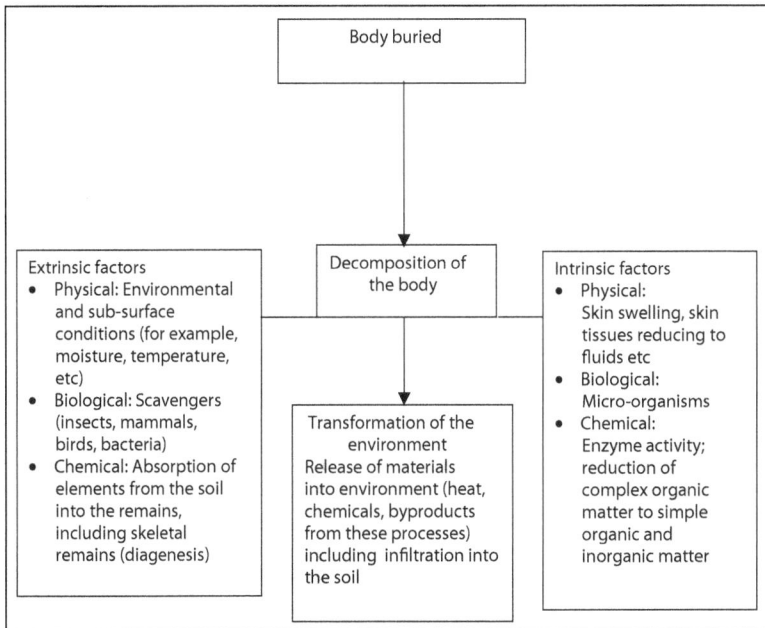

FIGURE 4.1
The grave and the decomposition of the body.

How might the soil within the grave (upcast) be different from surrounding soil? Factors suggested have been differences in temperature and pH (Rodriguez & Bass, 1985), higher levels of ionised water in disturbed soil (which may produce slightly increased current flow) (Owsley, 1995) and differences in electrical and magnetic stratification compared with the surrounding soil (Bevan, 1991; Owsley, 1995). These differences may be directly related to the creation of a grave and/or the presence of a body and its resultant decomposition.

Chemical Traces of the Buried Body in Soil

The chemical transformations the buried body undergoes are influenced by subsurface conditions. For example, when there is a sequence of wet and dry conditions (either seasonally or sporadically), organic materials tend to oxidize or decompose. Organic compounds may be vertically mobilised, rearranged or even displaced. Consequently, pH, calcium carbonate, organic matter and phosphate values 'will eventually be changed, distorted, or otherwise rendered meaningless' (Butzer, 1982, p. 116). Organic matter, potassium and nitrogen are incrementally destroyed or flushed out of the horizon. Phosphates, however, may change from soluble to fixed forms or may descend to lower soil horizons (Butzer, 1982).

It might be expected that elements of the body may be identified within burial soil. Phosphorus is a component of nervous tissue, bones and cell protoplasm, and increased levels of soil phosphorous have been found in the soils immediately surrounding a buried body, up to 10 cm below the body in Yorkshire (Chamberlain, 1994).

There are differing views as to how the alkalinity in the soil close to the body changes as a result of a decomposing body. It has been stated that soil pH indicates the presence of decompositional by-products (Vass et al., 1992) and there will be an increase in alkalinity (Imaizumi, 1974). In contrast, others state there will be reduced soil pH (Owsley, 1995; Garland & Janaway, 1989; Pate, Hutton, & Norrish, 1989). However, Garland & Janaway add that with the initial increase in acidity of the soil, there is an increase in buffering capacity, and more ionic charge groups of all kinds are produced that have the effect of cancelling any real change in pH. On the other hand, Mann et al. (1990) state the effect of soil pH is unknown in terms of the decomposition of the body itself.

Distinct patterns in the soil solution for volatile fatty acids during decomposition and for specific anions and cations once skeletonisation has occurred have been found (Vass et al., 1992). Seven ions investigated in this study proved useful due to their stability in the environment.

These were: sodium, chloride, ammonium, potassium, calcium, magnesium and sulphate (1992). Sulphate remained present in large amounts after 4 years. Calcium demonstrated a cyclic release from skeletal material that was found in substantial quantities. During decomposition, propionic, butyric and valeric acids (not the only ones formed) are formed and deposited in soil solution in specific ratios (Vass et al., 1992). Pfeiffer, Milne, & Stevenson (1998) identified the saturated fatty acids found in the highest proportion to be palmic acid (16:0) and stearic acid (18:0).

Longer-term (and more historical) burials show indicative traces in soil. For example, research from Bethell and Carver (1987) at the Sutton Hoo ship (unearthed in 1939) provided significant data linking chemical traces from the decomposition of bodies with inhumation sites over a long period of time. The Sutton Hoo was buried beneath a large raised mound (barrow) in East Anglia. The chemical traces of a human burial all occurred within a short distance (1–2 ft) of the site of the burial. Fourteen graves were excavated between 1984 and 1985, revealing a dark brown soil silhouette in the shape of human bones, contrasting with the lighter colour of the surrounding sand. Higher levels of copper, manganese and phosphorous were related to the presence of bone and the silhouette of bone compared with surrounding unstained soil. Boron, magnesium, nickel and zinc were also reported in the body silhouette. The burial silhouettes are stated as being formed from a combination of a mixture of residues from the burial itself (particularly skeletal phosphorous) and the additional biophile elements attracted from the surrounding soil matrix. Of the biophile elements, manganese was the most significant, causing the darker body 'stains'. The formation of body silhouettes/pseudomorphs in this case is a phenomenon of acid or sandy soils.

The development of field-friendly methods for indicative traces of buried human remains has yet to be researched and applied to forensic searches for graves.

Body Destruction by Grave Intruders

Besides decomposition within the grave, bodies may be destroyed by the intrusion into a grave of faunal scavengers. Temperature and weather will affect the extent and frequency of such intrusions. For example, colder weather reduces scavenging activity in areas where scavenging animals hibernate (Henderson, 1987). This type of scavenging can facilitate the body itself decomposing, because this allows access to the carcass by insects, as found by Turner and Wiltshire

(1999) in a study of buried pigs in the United Kingdom. The soil conditions at the research site (acidic, stagnogley soil, waterlogged and low in oxygen) and low temperatures had preserved the carcasses for three months before the onset of scavenging.

Skeletal Remains in the Burial Environment

When the soft tissues have decomposed, the skeleton is left in the burial environment. The bones and teeth are the most durable components of the body (Bass, 1987), but continue to be subject to environmental processes within the burial context (Boddington et al., 1987). This is the final stage of the decomposition of the buried corpse. The fundamental principles of post-mortem processes and their effect on bone are difficult to define, because of the many factors involved (Sandford, 1993). Bone is not immune to destructive conditions, although relatively little is known about processes that affect interred bone and the impact these have on the histological structure and preservation of skeletal remains (Garland, 1987; Cox & Bell, 1999).

Let us first be familiar with the nature of bone. Bone is made up of cells embedded in a calcified matrix; small reactive crystals of apatite within a matrix of collagen (Trueman, 2002). The matrix comprises organic materials that are principally collagen fibres and inorganic salts containing calcium and phosphate (Gray et al., 1995).

Bone may be dense (compact) or cancellous (trabecular or spongy) in texture. Compact bone is primarily found at the cortices of mature bone and cancellous bone lies in the interior of bones.

The inorganic phase of bone constitutes 70% of the weight, the organic phase 24% of the weight and the matrix water component of bone comprises 6% of the weight (Waldron, 1987). Approximately 5% is made up of glycoproteins (noncollagenous protein and carbohydrate; Gray et al., 1995). The organic phase of bone consists of collagen (Waldron, 1987) and comprises the elements carbon, nitrogen, hydrogen and oxygen (Pate & Hutton, 1988; Chamberlain, 1994). The inorganic phase is composed predominantly of crystals known as hydroxyapatite. The principal chemical elements of the inorganic or mineral phase are calcium, phosphorous and oxygen (Pate & Hutton, 1988).

Factors Affecting the Decomposition of Bone

Changes to bone after death are mainly caused by chemical erosion and this occurs in most environments. Chemical deterioration is accelerated by extremes of pH or by higher temperatures (Collins, Nielson-Marsh, Hiller, Smith, & Roberts, 2002). Factors impacting on the extent and type of erosion are the levels of acidity in the soil, the state of the body at burial (including bone density and age), moisture levels within the burial environment and the way in which the body is buried (Krogman & Iscan, 1986; Ubelaker & Scammell, 1992).

During burial, the transformations that occur to bone are:

- an uptake of cations and circulating organics
- an exchange of some ions
- the breakdown and leaching of collagen
- microbial intrusion and destruction
- changes to and possible leaching of the mineral matrix, and the deposition of minerals (Hedges, 2002).

Bone decomposition occurs when organic and inorganic components of bone become separated from each other and are destroyed. Physical and chemical factors within the burial environment remove the separated components of bone. Garland (1987) terms this process 'weathering'. Collagen is vulnerable to biodeterioration after the dissolution of the mineral component (Collins et al., 2002). The level of collagen content in bone decreases the longer a body is buried (Collins et al., 2002).

After the decomposition of the soft tissues of the body, the skeletal remains begin to exfoliate (McGregor et al., 1996). Microbes (bacteria, fungi and protozoa) are a primary agent in the first stages of the degradation of bone (Trueman, 2002) and this occurs rapidly after death (Collins et al., 2002). This is because they demineralise bone and produce tunnels or borings within bone. Fungi perforate the hard tissue of the dead bone, causing its destruction and decomposition; this type of post-mortem bone destruction by microorganisms within soil occurs in most burials (Piepenbrink, 1986). Near neutral pH soil conditions promote microbial activity, which would ordinarily protect bone (Collins et al., 2002).

In a burial situation, protein in the organic phase of bone converts through hydrolysis to peptides, which then reduce to their constituent amino acids. Simultaneously in the inorganic phase, the crystalline matrix is rearranged. Through this action, the bone is weakened because the protein– mineral bond is weakened; ions are substituted, infiltrated and absorbed, and proteins and minerals are removed. The type of soil and level of moisture (for example, from groundwater) will affect the rate of hydrolysis, prompting these changes to bone (Garland, 1987; Henderson, 1987). Collagen and its protein fibres react with water in the soil over time, promoted by warmer temperatures (Chamberlain & Pearson, 2001).

Burial in a humid environment leaves the bones more susceptible to the physical and chemical actions of the environment compared with those buried in a dry environment (Garland, 1987). Moisture affects bone through the action of leaching, once the soft protective body tissues have been removed (Goffer, 1980; Schwartz, 1993). The leaching of minerals weakens bone, promoting its destruction through surrounding acidic soils and water (Schwartz, 1993).

The composition of soils surrounding the bones is in turn altered as a result of an exchange of elements between bone and the soil. For example, cations and anions (notably calcium and phosphate ions) are deposited into the soil through bone erosion (McGregor et al., 1996). Diagenesis is the term given to the postburial chemical alteration of bone, including the loss of and increases to biogenic concentrations. The absorption by skeletal remains of elements within the soil is affected by many factors (Pate & Hutton, 1988; Pate et al., 1989; Edward & Benfer, 1993; Radosevich, 1993; Sandford, 1993).

Diagenesis can be burial and site-specific, because of the considerable variation in soil chemistry (Sandford, 1993; Pate, 1997). The exchange of elements between bone and soil will be dependent on the composition of the soil (the pH level), the duration of burial and the level of acidity in the groundwater (Burton, Price, Cahue, & Wright, 2003).

The Preservation of Bone

Differences in soil type will affect the preservation of bone (Brothwell, 1965; Krogman & Iscan, 1986). Bone is better preserved in soils with a neutral or slightly alkaline pH, and is worse in acid conditions (Keeley, Hudson, & Evans, 1977; Chamberlain, 1994).

Acidic conditions may lead to an alteration in the elemental composition of the bones (Waldron, 1987). Trace elements are more mobile in acidic environments (Waldron, 1987). Acids in the soil may lead to the dissolution of the inorganic matrix of bone (Henderson, 1987) and it is not necessary that strong acidic conditions be present for this to occur (Brothwell, 1965; Janaway, 1996). Bones will decay in soils where there is low pH and repeated cycles of hydration and dehydration (Spriggs, 1989). Pickering and Bachman (1997) cite a grave in Japan (Island of Yap) dating from the end of World War II in which the skeleton had all but disintegrated after 35 years because of the highly acidic soil. The different colour of the soil had revealed the place of interment.

Dry, alkaline, calcium carbonate-based soils (soils with a high pH or calcareous) will act to preserve bones (Chamberlain, 1994). Such was the case in the sands at Mauer in Germany, where the fossil jaw of the Heidelberg Man was discovered (Brothwell, 1965).

The hydrology (and in particular, rainwater) of a burial site will impact on the preservation of buried bone. For example, bones resting above or around the water table (Collins et al., 2002).

Cox and Bell (1999) state that where the environment is more extreme, such as very alkaline or very acidic, bone will be less likely to survive. As most often environments are not so extreme one way or another, there are difficulties in predicting bone preservation (Cox & Bell, 1999). Radosevich (1993) goes further, stating the bones can be differentially geochemically altered at different levels within a burial and within a bone. The difficulty of predicting bone preservation is shown by an example of variation to what would be expected when during an exhumation the bones of a woman buried for 165 years were discovered in a graveshaft (3.5 ft depth). In well-drained sandy loam soil, the pH reading was 4.9–5.1, suggesting moderately acidic conditions, which is generally not considered ideal for the preservation of organic remains (Wu & Bellantoni, 2003). It points to the likely interaction of other factors in the burial environment.

The conditions of the burial environment will impact on the rate and extent of decomposition of bones and soft tissues in any given postburial time period. The most significant of these are moisture, temperature, depth of burial, soil type, insect and bacteria activity. A body buried in a shallow grave is likely to decompose relatively quickly compared with a body buried in a formal burial 6 feet under the ground. The decomposition process is inhibited if the body is buried with clothing or other wrappings.

Once the soft tissues covering the skeleton are decayed, bone is exposed to processes of degradation; acidic soils will act to dissolve the inorganic matrix of the hydroxyapatite and this produces a material that is susceptible to leaching. Alkaline soils, on the other hand, may be expected to better preserve the skeletal remains. The skeleton and teeth are more durable and will form the most solid components of the body that may remain to be detected within the soil, depending on burial conditions and particularly the length of time before grave detection. These more durable parts of the body, the bones and teeth, may adsorb some elements from the soil.

The deposition of elements within the soil is an area that could be further researched in terms of its nature and duration in order to use this information for clandestine grave detection. At present, soil analysis over a large prospective burial area is time-consuming and results are not readily available in the field.

In terms of detection methods, the subsurface changes to the burial environment that occur as a result of decomposition are the retention of moisture within the soil, changes to soil stratigraphy, changes to chemical composition of the burial area compared with adjacent areas, and the presence of bones and possibly clothing items. These factors impact on subsurface anomaly detection methods and are referred to again when we explore clandestine grave detection methods.

5

Police Investigations of Buried Bodies

Missing persons and suspected murders are addressed by publicly funded agencies. These are police services, which have sole authority to conduct investigations into situations that relate to a known or possible crime. Missing persons may be the victims of crime. Although involving specialists from anthropology, archaeology, geology and other fields has led to research into shallow buried bodies and the means of detection, we need to bear in mind that police continue to conduct their investigations outside of a research sphere. This chapter is concerned with the pragmatics of the police search to locate bodies that are not found at the scene of the crime, whose whereabouts are not known. Throughout this book, it is emphasised that there is no comprehensive system of data collection regarding clandestine graves.

As a key source of information about practices following a murder, Australian police jurisdictions were approached about, first, the number of cases in which searches had been conducted to locate a murder victim in investigations, and second, the most commonly used search techniques. The questions related to the periods 1995–2000 and 2000–2002.

The questions were presented as a survey. For police to complete the questionnaire, they had to search files manually as the items on the survey could not be extracted from police databases (not being systematically recorded). This type of information could potentially assist investigations if able to be readily retrieved and analysed. The Federal Bureau of Investigations in the United States has begun to gather such information for further exploration.

There are six states and two territories in Australia. Five of the seven relevant states and territories responded to the first survey and two states responded to the second survey. The response rate for the first survey was 71%, and 29% for the second survey.

For the period 1995–2000, the five responding police jurisdictions reported a total of 23 murder victims for whom searches were required because the place of burial was not immediately located. During 2000–2002, there were 11 murder victims reported as not having been immediately found for whom searches were conducted. This is quite a marked difference, because it indicates that in the second reporting period, half the number of body searches previously reported were conducted by just two states in a much smaller time frame (two years compared with the previous five-year period).

There was some disparity between reported cases and information provided about activity undertaken. One state advised they could add a further 10 bodies to their total number of murder victims not found, but these were still technically classified as missing persons. As other states presumably face the same issue, it is likely that the number of unfound bodies may in fact be higher across all jurisdictions (this aspect is further addressed in the discussion).

Further, as at 2000, there were 25 bodies that had not yet been located that had been victims of murder before 1995, according to responding police services. This suggests a considerable caseload for this type of investigation.

For the period 1995–2000, the greater proportion of the 23 murder victims (10, or 48%) were found within six months. Nine (43%) were located within three months. Within two years after searching began, two bodies were located; within three years, a further two bodies were found and within five years, five bodies were located.

TABLE 5.1
Method of Recovery and Detection 1995–2000

Method	Total for all states
Passers-by (accidentally)	15
Police ground search	11
Verbal information	13
Ground penetrating radar	0
Cadaver dogs	0
Aerial surveillance	0
Forward looking infrared (FLIR)	0
Other	1*

Note: *Through unplanned excavation works.

In the period 2000–2002, nine of the eleven survey-reported bodies not immediately found were recovered within six months of searching (82%). The two that were reported to have been located within five years indicate that these searches were initiated before 2000. There were four bodies that had not been found at the time of responding whose cases were initiated before 2000.

This response indicates that the most common methods of body location are discovery by other people, or through additional information presented that assisted with police location, or police ground search. These responses suggest that other techniques, such as geophysical remote sensing equipment, aerial surveillance, forward-looking infrared surveys and cadaver dogs, had either not been found to be successful or had not been used in this period — it is not known which is the case.

The responses here do not include those that have not yet been located, and may still remain in shallow graves. The numbers provided by police for each question did not equate with the total number of bodies requiring searches. This is because responses included all bodies found during this period rather than only those that required searches for clandestine graves. Another state did not account for all bodies located in terms of method of recovery. Other states reported on combined search methods.

Of the types of places where bodies were deposited, 10 bodies were found in the metropolitan area and 24 in the outer metropolitan or more remote areas in Australia. In the metropolitan area, four were either in a shallow grave or under groundcover, such as bushes. A further four bodies were found close to a road and may also have been in shallow graves (unspecified).

For those bodies that were placed in the outer metropolitan or more remote areas in Australia, 16 of the 24 reported in this question were found under trees or other foliage, and five bodies were in shallow graves.

Only one state successfully applied an instrument during an investigation. Ground penetrating radar (GPR) was successfully used to locate two bodies during 2000–2002. Police ground search resulted in three body locations, and five were accidentally found (passers-by). The majority of the 11 bodies were therefore accidentally found.

In the period 2000–2002, 13 bodies were reported to be located in the outer metropolitan area; of which, six were found under bushes, logs or trees; one was in a shallow burial and two were in a deep burial. Of the four found in the metropolitan area, two were close to a road and one was carefully disguised (one was not described). Again, the figures in the responses do not total the 11 bodies requiring searches documented in this period, as was found for responses for the period 1995–2000.

Most initially unlocated human remains were recovered during 1995 and 2000 through accidental discovery or police ground searches, with some substantial contribution from informants (verbal information). There are 15 counts for passers-by discovering a body, 11 counts of police ground search recovering a body, 13 counts of further verbal information assisting in the location of a body and one recovered inadvertently through excavation works.

The information from the survey strongly suggests underreporting; that is, there are a greater number of searches for hidden bodies and bodies recovered than are identified here. The response rate for the two surveys was incomplete and there are clearly inconsistencies found in the responses, that is, the figures reported. All police services did not confine their responses to those cases not initially located and requiring searches for the defined survey periods. This may be a fault in the survey design, although it has resulted in a broader number of cases being included in some questions and not others. In fact, there are several reasons to suggest that the reported figures are lower than might be the actual case:

1. Police necessarily record persons as missing in the first instance, in the absence of a body, unless there is significant evidence to prove they are dead.

2. To complete the survey, police officers had to manually collate the information by going back through individual files. Files may have been overlooked in the absence of a database from which queries of this nature could be entered and most often new or less experienced officers were asked to complete the survey.

3. The survey was not forwarded by individual jurisdictions to all branches to obtain complete jurisdictional data due to the logistics of providing a response to the survey. This related to the organisational structure of some police jurisdictions; it is likely the data that were provided in both surveys were underreported because not all case files were centralised, but were maintained in various branch offices. For example, Queensland is divided into regional areas and the Queensland Police did not consider it feasible for each region to go through their records.

4. Although the survey did not require the presentation of any confidential data, it is speculated there may have been a reluctance to include all relevant cases as it may have been interpreted as reflecting on police capabilities to find murder victims or providing information that may have been viewed as sensitive.

5. Unsuccessful searches were clearly not included in the responses, although two states commented that there were additional persons presumed dead that had not been found and cases of suspicious circumstances documented on file.

It is important to make the point that given the logistical problems in extracting the data, police services were extremely helpful in responding to this questionnaire and were genuinely interested in the research.

Of the 23 bodies identified in the first survey, 10 (almost half) were located within six months, and the remaining 13 took significantly longer (and two bodies reported by one state were not included at all in this response). Of searches commencing, two bodies were found within two years, four bodies within three years and five bodies within five years. One state omitted the length of time it took to recover the two bodies they documented as not being initially found. Figures given in some reponses outnumbered the cases cited by police.

Personal communications with each of the police services at the time verified that ground search was still the most common search technique used, because other methods have been little researched or verified as being reliable in Australia. Geophysical instruments were not reported as used successfully to locate a body between 1995 and 2000. However, GPR was reported as being successfully used during the 2000–2002 period to locate two bodies (for one case) and this reflects the growing exploration of geophysical instruments for this purpose.

It is inferred from these results that other possible methods, such as chemical analyses of soils, the soil probe, electrical resistivity or electrical conductivity, for example, have not been successfully applied in Australia by police or consultants engaged by police.

Most bodies for which searches took place during 1995 and 2000 were found in remote areas or the outer metropolitan vicinity. There were 24 recoveries of bodies in the outer metropolitan area compared with 10 in the metropolitan area. Combined with the outer metropolitan area, this presents a total of 34 bodies located between 1995 and 2000 (as noted, this is inconsistent with the total number of bodies requiring searches). Shallow burials were specifically documented for five of those 24 found in the outer metropolitan area; 16 recoveries were found under trees, logs or bushes; one close to a road; one carefully disguised (method not stated) and one in a mineshaft. Of the 10 bodies found in the metropolitan area, four were found close to the road, two were carefully disguised (details not stated), four were either located beneath trees, logs or bushes or in shallow burials.

In the absence of a substantial collection of literature on searches for clandestine graves in Australia, this survey of Australian police jurisdictions provides important information about how hidden human remains are most often located in practice. These figures are a small proportion of actual searches conducted due to the logistical constraints confronted by police in extracting this type of information. It does not reflect total cases in each state or territory. The number of unlocated bodies may in reality be much higher, as suggested by the additional suspicious cases cited by one state and those presumed dead quoted by another state. Certainly, these statistics do not include all cases of unlocated bodies, and officially persons remain classified as missing rather than dead. In Chapter 7 we will explore the places in which concealed bodies have been found, as reported in the media. During a four-year period, 184 bodies were reported in the Australian media as having been found, most in outer metropolitan areas described as bushland, national parks or reserves. It may be that a greater interface between police services and scientists would enhance searches for hidden bodies.

A Grave Research Site

Being able to flag potential surface signs of graves can save a great deal of time and expense. There is only a very small amount of information about what clandestine graves look like at different postburial intervals. There is less known about whether or not the observations from one environment type hold more or less true for other sites, accepting interceding variables. That environments differ means factual information gained from the observation of graves in varying landscapes is valuable to police and investigators. This chapter contains descriptions of graves in a scrubland setting at which surface appearances over several years were observed. The surface changes described here are useful for similar environments.

When I began my research in 1999, such forensic burial-oriented research studies had not been conducted in Australia for the purpose of locating clandestine graves. More specifically, there was no research-based documentation as to what clandestine graves might look like over an extended period of time. I therefore adopted the role of body disposer and 'recreated' clandestine graves containing animal and human burials.

Three kangaroos were buried first, followed by three pigs. The animal carcasses were relatively easy to obtain. Access to human cadavers for this type of new research took some considerable time (largely for procedural reasons). Donating individuals had full knowledge of the objects of the research and provided signed permission. These logistics contribute to the rarity of this type of research. The dates of burial are recorded in Table 6.1. For moral and ethical reasons, a wire cage was erected around the human gravesites to prevent animals from disturbing the human cadavers (which had been donated to the medical science research program). To increase the validity of the observations, all the graves were left undisturbed by people

TABLE 6.1
Date of Construction of Graves

Burial sequence (n)	Date of burial
Kangaroos (3)	March 1999
Pigs (3)	July 2000
Human body (1)	February 2002
Calibration pit (1)	January 2003
Human body (1)	March 2004

during the research period, and no chemicals were used on the burial areas during the period of this experiment.

Kangaroos have not previously been used in this type of experimental study. They were suitable for several reasons, not least of which was their availability. For the focus of this research, close anatomical similarity to humans was not essential. An advantage is that kangaroo skeletons contain long bones that may imitate any signature statements expected from human bones, unlike pigs that typically have shorter bones. The mass of a kangaroo is approximately equivalent to that of a human body, and different-sized kangaroos presented an opportunity to simulate the mass of a man, woman and child.

In contrast, pigs have been used to simulate human remains in graves because they are considered to be biochemically and physiologically similar enough to humans for studies about patterns and rates of decay, and scavenging. Mature pigs are similar to humans in weight (70 kg on average), have a similar fat-to-muscle ratio and, like humans, they do not have heavily haired skin. Pigs have been used in other studies relating to burials (e.g., France et al., 1992, 1997; Schultz et al., 2002).

The design, construction and placement of the gravesites were intended to replicate forensic scenarios, modelled on information from police officers and case studies. Therefore, all graves were dug using only shovels, spades and picks. The graves were relatively shallow; the depth of burial ranged from a maximum of 1 m to a minimum of 0.43 m. The environmental situations of the graves were varied to include burials near trees, in open flat areas and near logs or bushes. The remains (animal and human) were buried with a range of 'typical' artifacts, such as plastic bags or clothing items (synthetic and cotton, shoes and belts), or nothing.

Description of Burial Sites

The section of land in which the kangaroos and pigs were buried was a fenced area with restricted road access, north of Adelaide, the capital of

FIGURE 6.1
Burial area of kangaroos and pigs. The area selected for the kangaroo and pig burials, showing the fenceline to the left, demarcates the scrubland from the cropped area. This view is looking south.

South Australia (see Figure 6.1). It is representative of typical open scrubland in a semi-arid country. Overall, the site contained grassy undergrowth, was lightly wooded with native gum trees, and had fallen tree timber littered about.

So that this burial research may be used in search cases or to compare with other studies in semi-arid environments, some details about the area are included here. This part of Australia is classified as arid or semi-arid. Its Mediterranean climate has hot dry summers from December through to February and cool winters during June through to August. Most rainfall occurs during the winter period (the annual rainfall in this zone is 450–525 mm). The altitude is 78 m.

The burial area is a plain with gentle slopes and deep, inherently fertile, moderately drained soils. There are no standing water or creek beds in the vicinity. The underlying sediments are classified as Quaternary (believed to be younger than 1 million years). The geology comprises alluvial clays, mantled by a veneer of fine-grained carbonates of aeolian origin. There are hard-setting surfaces and some poorly structured subsoils. The three soil horizons (termed A, B and C) are calcareous (solonised brown soil);

an alkaline soil with underlying carbonate-based soil geology. The soils are neutral to slightly alkaline at the surface, and alkaline to strongly alkaline with depth.

Predominantly, there were shrubs and groundcover in the area. The dominant vegetation type is the mallee box (*Eucalyptus porosa*) and other various mallee types, such as black box and white mallee trees. Other canopy species are the *Callitris pressii*. The dominant groundcover (shrub) is the *Rhagodia parabolica* (a saltbush). The grasses are the *Stipa* (spear-grasses) and weeds, such as Paterson's curse (*Echium plantagineum,* also known as Viper's Bugloss or Salvation Jane).

The human bodies were buried at the back of a cemetery for protection purposes, in the same geographical zone as the animal burial site. Here again, the ground is flat and relatively even with no waterways. The natural vegetation was cleared as part of the cemetery property. The pre-dominant vegetation types were low growing, introduced groundcover species, including soursob (*Oxalis pes-caprae*) and Salvation Jane.

Construction of the Burial Sites

The three kangaroos varied in size and weight and were selected to be rep-resentative in mass of an adult human male, female and child — a large red male kangaroo, aged approximately 15 years; a large grey kangaroo, slightly smaller than the red kangaroo, aged approximately 10 years; and a small grey kangaroo, aged approximately 2 years. They were frozen on col-lection and were buried on the same day. An average adult male kangaroo

TABLE 6.2
Depth and Contents of Kangaroo Graves

Site	Burial depth	Kangaroo type	Site description	Grave contents
1	1.0 m	Slightly smaller grey kangaroo. Age approximately 10 years.	Open flat area	Contained a denim dress woollen jumper, with metal buttons, a cotton socks and a leather belt.
2	0.75 m	Large red kangaroo. Age approx 15 years.	Adjacent to fallen logs	Contained a pair of cotton trousers, a nylon shirt and a plastic belt with a metal buckle.
3	0.59 m	Small grey kangaroo. Age approx 2 years.	At base of tree	Contained a pair of cotton jeans, socks, a nylon scarf, cotton shirt, a cloth (material) belt. A large plastic garbage bag was placed on top of the kangaroo.

FIGURE 6.2
Pig burial area. It shows the pigs in ziplock bags and implements used to prepare the graves. The kangaroos were buried behind the two leaning trees in the centre of the photograph. The scene depicts the usual winter vegetation for the area and is taken viewing south.

weighs between 50–90 kg, depending on type, and females can weigh between 20–35 kg.

Burying the kangaroos proved to be a difficult task. For one thing, the graves were dug during summer and the ground was extremely hard. Further, the kangaroos were frozen at the time of burial, limiting the way in which they could be laid into the grave. They were laid out full length in the grave and turned on one side. Due to the irregular shape and frozen nature of the tail, these were sawn off and placed inside the graves.

The nomenclature used for the animal graves was straightforward: kangaroo sites 1, 2 and 3; and pig sites 1, 2 and 3. Kangaroo site 1 contained a large adult-sized (gray) kangaroo and was situated in the middle of the grid in an open, flat area with no trees or shrubs at a depth was 1.0 m. Kangaroo site 2 contained the largest kangaroo and was situated between two fallen logs at a depth of 0.75 m. Kangaroo site 3 was located at the base of a gum tree and contained the smallest kangaroo and was buried at a depth of 0.59 m. The minimum distance between each grave was 6 m. Within each grave, items of clothing as might be found on humans were included in the burials (as stated in Table 6.2).

Three pigs were buried in an area adjacent to the kangaroos, approximately 20 m away. All three pigs were evenly sized, each weighing approximately 60 kg. Their length was 1.1 m and they were aged 18 weeks. The pigs were stored in a cold room in plastic bags (not frozen) for one day until burial, shown in Figure 6.2.

The burial schema was the same as that adopted for the kangaroos for comparative reasons; one in an open flat area, one near a low growing bush and the third at the base of a large mature gum tree (see Table 6.3). Overall, the area in which the pigs were buried had more vegetation (grass, shrubs and Salvation Jane) coverage than the kangaroo area.

The pigs were buried in July 2000, a winter month in South Australia. Unlike the experience with burying the kangaroos (which occurred during summer), the topsoil was relatively soft from the rains. Due to an underlying limestone layer that was difficult to penetrate using shovels, picks and spades, the average depth of these graves was limited to 0.5 m.

TABLE 6.3
Depth and Contents of Pig Graves

Site	Burial depth	Length/width	Site description	Grave contents
1	0.50 m	1.6 × 0.7m	Open flat area	Unclothed, inside an unsealed black large garbage bag.
2	0.43 m	1.3 × 0.7m	Near low bush	Clothed, consisting of white cotton knitted top, purple cotton track pants, cotton socks, black rubber-soled sandshoes (Nike brand), vinyl brown belt with metal buckle.
3	0.50 m	1.4 × 0.7m	At base of tree	Clothed in a white cotton sundress, no shoes.

TABLE 6.4
Depth and Contents of Human Body Graves and Calibration Pit

Site	Burial depth	Length/width	Grave contents
1	0.75 m	1.5 × 1.0m	Elderly woman. Clothing consisted of underwear and a loose cotton nightgown, no shoes or jewellery.
2	0.8 m	1.65 × 0.8m	Elderly woman. No other articles.
3	0.59 m	0.95 × 1.7m	Calibration pit. No contents.

The burial contents and grave dimensions of the human graves and calibration pit are given in Table 6.4.

Burying the human bodies was approached somewhat differently to the animals. Prior to burying the human bodies, a protective cage had been erected using metal poles and meshed wire that measured 4 m wide and 6 m long. Wire mesh was also laid over the top, creating a permeable roof, leaving a standing height of approximately 2 m. Around the base of the cage, strong wire mesh was pinned to the ground to prevent scavenging animals from digging underneath the cage. It was designed to prevent foxes in particular, or any other animals from disturbing the grave for ethical purposes (given that the graves contained human bodies). Clandestine burials of murder victims obviously would not have this protection. The size of the cage allowed for standing area (see Figure 6.3) and also protected the natural vegetation growth within the cage from being mown by groundskeepers.

The first human body for a study of this nature in Australia was buried within the cage (forefront of Figure 6.3) during summer. This meant it was time consuming and difficult to dig the hardened ground using shovels, spades and picks.

FIGURE 6.3
Protective cages containing human bodies. The first human cadaver buried is in the foreground. The second body was buried in the cage behind. The view is looking south.

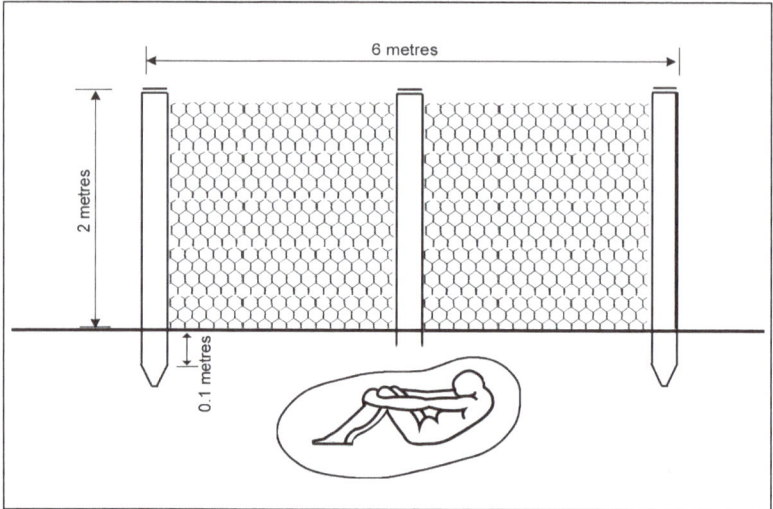

FIGURE 6.4
Diagram of the cage and position of human body 1. The arrow at the bottom indicating 0.1m represents the wire mesh laid out on the surface around the cage.
Note: Figure not to scale.

FIGURE 6.5
Second human burial (March 2004). The surrounding mound of soil is shown in the foreground. This view is facing north.

The body was that of an elderly woman, who had died 3 days before and weighed approximately 52–56 kg. The body was not treated (embalmed) in any way before burial. The burial position was flexed, in a semifoetal position, and lying on one side to accommodate the dimensions of the grave (Figure 6.4). Clothing consisted of underwear and a loose cotton nightgown. Upcast soil was replaced over the body and smoothed over on the surface using the shovels. The darker-coloured and more rubbly upcast clearly demarcated the gravesite and this area of upcast at the surface measured 3.3 by 2 m.

The second burial took place 2 years later in the adjacent caged area. The distance between the two human graves was approximately 2.5 m. The body was that of an elderly woman (aged 82 years) weighing approximately 55 kg. She was buried in a semiflexed position. No clothing or other articles were included. To vary the landscape, a circular mound of soil was piled around the grave as a catchment for water, to examine any effect on plant growth and soil consolidation. The extra soil had been obtained from the same area to create the mound. When the grave was complete, the surface was slightly higher than the surrounding area as can be seen in Figure 6.5.

A calibration pit (or empty control grave) was prepared outside the caged area at the end of the row of three cages, as there was no reason to provide protection from scavenging. The process was straightforward; the soil was dug out of a hole to create the grave, then refilled and the surface smoothed.

Surface Appearance of Graves

After creating the replication clandestine graves, the ground surface was carefully observed over the next several years. The surface aspects of any change to the landscape can be observed most readily through the presence of insects, the activity of animals, plant regrowth or destruction and changes to the soil surface (through wind, additional elements to the soil, heat and cold). Each of these aspects is described in connection to the clandestine graves under observation.

Insect Activity

Entomologists have studied insect activity as it relates to decomposition and this is an important source of information for estimating time since death. However, the focus here was whether the presence of insects served to indicate likely gravesites in ways that stood out from insect activity in other nearby areas of the gravesites. It was found that at the surface of the gravesites, there was relatively little direct observable insect activity over a prolonged period. Surface insect activity (ants and blowflies) was observed around the kangaroo and pig gravesites only during the first 12 months of burial and appeared to be seasonally related, that is, noticeable in the warmer months. During winter periods, there was no insect activity recorded.

At the surface, only ants and blowflies were sighted. At the animal gravesites, ants and blowflies (large blue-black flies) were found around all gravesites up to 13 months post burial. Beetle shells were found on one kangaroo grave surface (site 1) at 10 weeks postburial and 'ticks' were found around the gravesites at 13 months. There was relatively continuous ant activity at pig site 1, because it had been buried on an ant site, but at the other two pig gravesites ant activity was not particular to the graves during the observation period. After just over 2 years (27 months), no ants were appearing around the kangaroo gravesites.

Interestingly, on the surface of the human gravesites there was no particular insect activity seen during monitoring periods, including the calibration pit. Although blowflies were present in summer periods, they were no more numerous at the gravesite areas than the wider burial area. In practical search terms, in these circumstances insect activity would not serve as a key indicator of a burial unless a professional entomologist was involved, and the search was conducted within the first few months of burial.

Faunal Activity

Animal burrowing proved to be an obvious and unsubtle sign of a burial. Larger animals (foxes) interfered with the animal burial sites and this occurred soon after burial, and continued intermittently over several years. Scavenging did not appear to be seasonally related, because it occurred both in summer and winter. This of course was prevented at the human graves by the protective cage and there were no signs of digging at the calibration site, as was expected. The only indications of faunal activity at the human sites were rabbit droppings at the calibration pit.

The patterns of grave scavenging were similar at all animal gravesites and suggested the same type of animals were responsible on each occasion, namely foxes, which are the common predators in the area. Foxes (*Vulpes vulpes*), introduced to Australia in the 1850s, are prevalent in South Australia and are closely correlated with the presence of rabbits (Department of Environment and Heritage, 2003). The European rabbit (*Oryctolagus cuniculus*) is found throughout most parts of South Australia and are a food source for high numbers of foxes and feral cats. In terms of the environment, rabbits limit the regeneration of native vegetation because they feed on seedlings.

The animal digging significantly impacted on the surface appearance of the gravesites, which soon bore no resemblance to the original graves. Disturbed by burrowing, the graves were subject to weathering. This led to the overhanging edges of the graves that had been burrowed out to collapse. Sharp, dug-out edges were smoothed by natural processes and the hole appeared after time passed as a scooped out shallow, possibly easy to miss in a search.

The pattern of burrowing is described in the following passages for the kangaroo and pig graves. At the kangaroo sites, burrowing had occurred soon after burial (within 1 month), with large holes being dug to an approximate depth of 0.3 m. The first diggings at the gravesites are shown in Figures 6.6, 6.7 and 6.8. These first burrows comprised single large holes dug at sites 1 and 2 and three smaller holes at site 3. The most startling effect was this burrowing altered the surface appearance of the graves, so that the gravesites looked like burrows rather than 'graves'. At different stages over 5 years, various disarticulated bone sections were found near the gravesites, stripped of flesh.

FIGURE 6.6
Kangaroo site 1, first incidence of burrowing (April, 1999). This is viewing eastwards.

FIGURE 6.7
Kangaroo site 2, first incidence of burrowing (April, 1999). This is facing south-west.

FIGURE 6.8
Kangaroo site 3, first incidence of burrowing (April, 1999). Photograph faces west.

FIGURE 6.9
Pig site 1. Early post-burial burrowing (September, 2000). Photograph faces south.

The pig burials were also interfered with by animals (foxes) within a few weeks of interment and during the first year of burial, and then again at 3–4 years of burial. Large holes had been dug at the centre of all three graves, the foxes having easily reached the pigs' shallow buried remains. The soil at this stage was soft from having been recently overturned. At site 1, the pig skull was exposed. At site 2, the plastic bag in which the pig had been placed was ripped open and shreds of plastic were around the grave. At site 3, the digging had exposed the clothing on the pig body.

In the first 12-month period following burial, all three pig sites were burrowed a second time at 3 months (September 2000) and a third time at 4 months after burial (October 2000) and, later, 7 months after burial (January 2001). Figures 6.9, 6.10 and 6.11 show the features of the second burrowing incidents. At this time, the skull of pig 1 was found disarticulated away from the grave with the mandible separated and lying close by the grave. Clothing and bones were found near the gravesites. However, there were no observed signs of further digging and no bones were found near site 3.

Burrowing and scavenging continued over several years, but in a halting fashion as the foxes returned for food. After the first occasion of

FIGURE 6.10
Pig site 2. Early post-burial burrowing (September, 2000). Photograph faces north.

FIGURE 6.11
Pig site 3. Early post-burial burrowing (September, 2000). Photograph faces north.

FIGURE 6.12
Kangaroo site 2. After further burrowing in February 2004.

burrowing soon after burial, two of the kangaroo graves (sites 1 and 2) were not burrowed again until 5 years later, probably because of the attraction of nearby pig sites. At this later stage, they were burrowed three times in a 12-month period (2004). When the kangaroos had been buried for 5 years, a long tunnel was dug into sites 1 and 2, which completely altered the appearance of the grave surfaces. Notably, both the kangaroo and pig sites located at the base of trees (sites 3) remained relatively undisturbed by the foxes following an initial dig.

The later diggings at kangaroo sites 1 and 2 resulted in fresh upcast piled around the gravesites. A fox had made its home in one burrow and was seen bounding out. Site 3 continued to not be disturbed. Subsequent burrowing a few months later led to the entrance to the burrow collapsing. As a result of these disturbances, the graves' surfaces looked like scooped out depressions in the soil, such as might be man-made for building a campfire.

The pig sites, like the kangaroo sites, were also burrowed at later postburial stages (after 3 years, 3.5 years and 4 years). The pig buried under the tree (site 3) was significantly less disturbed. This grave had thick debris and bark over the surface.

FIGURE 6.13
Kangaroo site 2 after further borrowing in June 2004.

FIGURE 6.14
Pig site 1. After further burrowing in June 2004. Bones dragged from the middle of the grave are scattered on the surface near the grave. Photograph faces west.

The foxes did not remove the bones far from the graves. These findings suggest that bones removed from graves by foxes are likely to be very near the buried remains. Other scavengers might be inclined to take foraged bones further from the actual burial.

In terms of surface appearance, the burrows formed a catchment for fallen plant litter.

Plant Regrowth

The next surface feature described from direct observation of graves is vegetation or plant coverage of the graves. As would be expected, immediately after the graves were dug, the breaks in the vegetation caused by the graves (and presence of upcast) were obvious (see Figure 6.15). This is the easiest time to locate a grave, providing devious persons do not mask or cover it.

What subsequently grows on the upcast is of interest as potential distinguishing characteristics. After some months, vegetation patterns at the gravesites revealed:

- the plants that were first to grow after the graves were created (successional growth) tended to be local hardy weeds

FIGURE 6.15
Pig site 3 at burial (July 2000). Photograph faces east.

- there was no diversity between the plants that grew on and around the graves and the general surrounds
- there were distinct seasonal growth patterns
- the position of the grave in relation to surrounding land features influenced vegetation growth.

The usual seasonal patterns of vegetation growth at the animal burial area comprised the grass (*Stipa*) dying off in the summer seasons, and soursob and sporadic Salvation Jane regrowing thickly and densely during the winter season. During summer, the heat and aridity dried off most of the grass and low ground cover growth, and the upcast of the graves could be readily identified. In each successive winter period, extensive ground cover obscured the graves. Climate was seen to strongly influence vegetation growth over the gravesites, which varied with seasonal fluctuations. It is important to note that intermittent burrowing by scavengers impacted on the ability of the vegetation to be sustained and regrow undisturbed at the animal gravesites.

The first winter rains after burial precipitated sparse regrowth directly over the graves, and sparse vegetation growing on all areas of upcast. Weed varieties, rather than native plants, grew first on and around the gravesites. Soursob was the first successional plant to grow near the gravesites, noticeably in winter; grasses (typical of the area) grew during summer, and a scattering of Salvation Jane grew near the graves. These plants could be sustained by the upcast, at least initially. All the plants that grew on or near the graves during the observation period were commonly found in the surrounding areas. Upcast was not conducive to the long-term growth of many plants, particularly in summer, and those most resilient were the soursob and Salvation Jane.

The soursob was hardy enough, with a shallow root system, to be the first successional plant over upcast. Soursob grows in mid-autumn from tuberous roots and bulbils beneath the ground. The leaves are bright green and groups of yellow flowers grow from a single flower stem. In South Australia, soursob reproduces vegetatively through the underground bulbilis, and its spread is aided by soil disturbances. When dense, the exclusion of light from the soil surface inhibits the growth of almost all plants beneath it. As a result, the soil is bare in summer after the soursob has died back (Allanson, 2004). This effect was observed at all gravesites.

No new plant varieties appeared. Plant regrowth on or near the gravesites was limited to grass, soursob and Salvation Jane; that is, the same plant types as were growing in the burial areas. During winter, the vegetation common to the field (soursob and Salvation Jane) covered the area, except for the holes burrowed by animals, and this winter growth obscured the grave holes from sight.

As each summer season commenced, there were areas around the graves characterised by a lack of vegetation growth that roughly followed the placement of upcast. These 'halo' or necrotic barren areas were larger at the kangaroo graves compared with the pig graves. These were the first noticeable distinguishing features at the gravesites.

After the first postburial winter, there were areas around all six animal gravesites in which there was no vegetation growth (termed 'halos' here). In subsequent summer periods, kangaroo sites 1 and 2 had areas around the gravesites in which no vegetation grew over 6 years. The halo effect, in varying degrees, of no vegetation during summer was observed soon after burial and corresponded with the placement of the upcast. This arid, cracked, necrotic zone persisted each summer at kangaroo sites 1 and 2, and was clearly visible because ground litter did not tend to settle on these barren areas over the 6-year monitoring period. Little or no groundcover grew within approximately 1.5 m around kangaroo site 1, although there were sprigs of new grass growing at the edges of the holes only. The boundary of the halo area was where high, dead, yellow grass grew. At this point, away from the gravesite, the grasses and ground cover grew as elsewhere in the field.

In terms of grave recovery, these graves did not regain their postburial appearance and featured minimal groundcover, such as leaves and gumnuts, compared with surrounding areas. The two animal sites under the trees (kangaroo and pig sites 3) did, however, regain more of a preburial appearance after 3 years due to the deposit of ground litter, growth of grasses during the summer period that was typical of the surrounding area and the site itself before burial, and of course, not being burrowed by animals as often. The details of this plant growth over the gravesites is shown in the photographs of the gravesites in this section.

Figures 6.16 and 6.17 show kangaroo site 1 during the first autumn, and then the first winter after burial. The gravesite is visible because of the bare upcast at this interim season and initial sparseness of plant growth (Figure 6.16). Three months after the kangaroos had been interred, the area was covered in the winter ground cover (soursob plants; Figure 6.17). As winter advanced, there was thick ground coverage as soursob grew over the entire area. The soursob plants did not grow in the middle of the burrowed area, but the nearby coverage was dense enough to obscure the burrowed area from easy viewing. Each winter season, the soursob

FIGURE 6.16
Kangaroo site 1 (April 1999). Photograph faces south. The arrow points to the gravesite.

FIGURE 6.17
Kangaroo site 1 (June 1999). Photograph faces south. The arrow points to the gravesite.

FIGURE 6.18
Kangaroo site 1 (October 1999). The photograph faces west.

FIGURE 6.19
Kangaroo site 1 (December 1999). The photograph shows the halo formed around the grave in which there is no vegetation growth. The photograph faces southeast.

obscured sighting the graves readily, as it grew on the surrounding ground up to the edges of the holes dug by scavengers. At such times, there appeared to be no visible difference in the plant cover over the area, and the graves could only be located by finding the holes in which the groundcover was not growing. As the climate became drier and warmer, grasses around the grave flattened and died.

Although the principal plants in the area grew according to season around the edges of the burrows 1 month after burial, they did not begin to grow from the centre of the burrow holes until 3 to 4 years after burial of the animals, despite the presumed collection of water within the burrowed animal gravesites. In winter periods, the vegetation was actually growing from the upper edges of the gravesites, serving to cover the holes from sight.

Figure 6.18 shows fresh grass growing close to the grave edges and on the upcast surrounding the gravesite following the first winter after burial. Between the gravesite and the nearest grasses is a considerable gap. This circular area around site 1 remained sparsely vegetated during each successive summer (dry) period and is more sharply defined in Figure 6.19, which shows kangaroo site 1 and its bare surround during the summer period nearly 1 year after burial. The animal burrowing distinguishes the gravesite. Figure 6.20 shows kangaroo site 1 after almost 3 years at the height of summer, showing the barren nature of the immediate grave surrounds.

This early postburial vegetation pattern applied to the pig gravesites, despite being buried in the opposite season to the kangaroos. Vegetation did not grow within the gravesites until after 3 years and there was an absence of debris or ground litter at the animal sites, indicating disturbed soil.

During the summer period in the first year of the pig burials (at 6 months after burial), a 0.5 m radius of no vegetation growth was observed around pig site 1 (see Figure 6.21). At pig site 1 (buried in an open, flat area), there was only one area at the southern end where there was minimal plant growth that coincided with the presence of upcast and this area continued to show this halo effect of flattened and sparse grass for 5 years (Figure 6.23). The upcast, however, continued to be visible through the plant growth. The bare area coincided with where the majority of the upcast had been placed during burial.

At pig site 2, the area of no vegetation or flattened grass fanned out, away from the sheltering bush, again coinciding with the placement of upcast during burial. After 3 years, the halo had extended to 2 m. In

FIGURE 6.20
Kangaroo site 1 (January 2002). The photograph faces east.

FIGURE 6.21
Pig site 1 showing halo (January 2001). Photograph faces north east.

FIGURE 6.22
Pig site 1 after 2.5 years (February 2003). Photograph faces east.

FIGURE 6.23
Pig site 1 (October 2005). Photograph faces east.

FIGURE 6.24
Pig site 2 showing a halo (January 2001). Photograph faces north.

FIGURE 6.25
Pig site 2 (January 2001). This photograph features a close up of the halo. The view faces north.

FIGURE 6.26
Pig site 2 after 3 years (February 2003). Photograph faces north.

interim seasons, the halo was characterised by flattened grass that was dying off. The end of the halo was signified by grass standing tall, as shown in Figure 6.27. The flattened grass suggests growth that could not be sustained over the upcast.

Figure 6.27 shows the halo effect and its extent (at site 2), as the grass begins to die off coincident with the upcast.

Site 3, located under the tree, only featured a limited halo effect at 1 year after burial (May 2001), when a small radius of no plant growth was noted. After this time, no evidence of even a small halo was observed.

The reason for this halo effect is more likely to be a result of upcast being brought to the surface and providing a base for growth for introduced weed species, or shallow-rooted plants not surviving the summer periods. Exposed or disturbed soil surfaces may be subject to rain, which can be damaging because the force of impact breaks up aggregates, thereby facilitating the washing of particles into more 'closer packing'. A cap that forms on the soil surface reduces seedling re-emergence and the rate at which water enters the soil is reduced, and may also cause run-off and erosion (Rowell, 1994). In addition, the soursob plant type that grew on this soil has the effect of creating barren areas in its wake. It is proba-

FIGURE 6.27
Pig site 2 (October 2005). Photograph faces north.

FIGURE 6.28
Figure 33: Kangaroo site 1 (October 2005). The arrow points to the grave. Photograph faces east.

ble that this effect would be seen at other gravesites with similar surrounds, especially in South Australia given the prevalence of the soursob weed. Hunter (1996) states that in drought or dry environmental conditions, any vegetation growing in areas that do not retain moisture will parch more quickly. This is supported by the halos of no growth found in this research.

Figure 6.28 (kangaroo site 1 after 6 years of burial) shows growth in an interim season. Prolonged rains sustained vegetation, after which the area became bare once again. The burial is located in the centre of the photograph where the taller grasses are situated, obscuring the burrow.

At kangaroo site 2, there was a 2-metre half-circular halo at one end in which there was no vegetation and no ground litter. At the other end was a log. This radius of no vegetation regrowth (where the upcast had been placed) measured 0.4 m after almost 3 years (32 months). In contrast, the pattern at kangaroo site 3 showed a halo area of 1.5 m at 7 months postburial. This decreased to 0.8 m after almost 2 years and after nearly 3 years (32 months) postburial there was no halo at this site because debris was now masking this grave. However, there were bare patches of ground around the grave area.

Kangaroo sites 1, 2 and 3 (Figures 6.29, 6.31 and 6.32) photographs show how regrowth of the ground cover remains sparse over the gravesite compared with the surrounds after 4 years. Figure 6.30 shows site 2 as the winter grass begins to die off, and the grass away from the log is sparse and flattened. The burrow is obscured by the tall grasses growing from the middle of the grave area.

Aside from ground cover and weeds, only one new plant was observed to grow at any of the gravesites; at kangaroo site 1, a small saltbush grew at the edge of grave.

Along with the vegetation, natural ground litter is cleared when graves are created. Although leaves and gumnuts collected in the centre of all three grave burrows (from the scavenging), ground litter notably did not collect on the upcast around the graves during the first few months postburial; in fact, ground litter was minimal after 6 years. Its reappearance was quicker at both kangaroo and pig sites 3, most likely because they were located beneath trees, a natural source of the 'litter', and such debris began to collect close to these gravesites after 6–10 months. The minimal ground litter at kangaroo site 1 is shown in Figure 6.31, 4 years after burial. The difference in the colour of the upcast from the surface soil in the area is also visible when there is minimal vegetation and groundcover.

FIGURE 6.29
Kangaroo site 2 vegetation (May 2003).

FIGURE 6.30
Kangaroo site 2 (October 2005). The photograph faces north east.

FIGURE 6.31
Kangaroo site 1 May 2003.

FIGURE 6.32
Kangaroo site 3 vegetation in May 2003. Photograph faces southwest.

FIGURE 6.33
Kangaroo site 3 (October 2005). Photograph faces west.

FIGURE 6.34
Pig site 3 (January 2001). Photograph faces north.

FIGURE 6.35
Pig site 3 (January 2001). Photograph faces west.

FIGURE 6.36
Pig site 3 (January 2002). Photograph faces north.

FIGURE 6.37
Pig site 3 after 2.5 years (February 2003). Photograph faces west.

FIGURE 6.38
Pig site 3 (October 2005). Photograph faces north.

In comparison, Figure 6.32 at kangaroo site 3 shows a higher degree of ground litter around the grave and base of the tree due to the nearby tree. Here, soursob is growing close to the burrowed areas, perhaps because of water catchment. Figure 6.33 shows kangaroo site 3 after 6 years of burial, towards the left of the photograph at the base of the tree. There is a thick layer of ground litter over the grave and at this stage the grave was largely indistinguishable from the surrounding mottled growth.

Figures 6.34–6.38 show the 'recovery' of pig site 3. Although there is bare ground in two photographs (Figures 6.34 and 6.35), this shows the burrowing and the grass is growing up to the edges of the grave. Site 3 was the first grave to 'recover' from the disturbance and become completely masked by vegetation that was undifferentiated from the surrounds at 12 months postburial. By 18 months postburial, the site had returned to its preburial appearance except for the hole, although the hole was difficult to discern at that stage (Figure 6.36). By the close of the monitoring period, pig site 3 was largely indistinguishable from the surrounds, because of ground litter (Figure 6.38). Figure 6.37 in particular shows the extent of site recovery after 2.5 years of burial.

An aside was that during winter, no moss grew near or on the grave areas when it was growing in other parts of the same area. This continued over the 6 years of monitoring, although moss was found in the broader area. It is probable that this is related to the composition of the upcast scattered around the surface of the grave areas. After disturbance to the soil crust (e.g., through stock trampling), studies of the growth of lichens and mosses on the Australian biological soil crust indicate it may take 30 to 40 years to achieve predisturbance vegetation cover levels (Eldridge and Kinnell, 1997). When soil crusts have been destroyed, natural regeneration is slow.

Human Graves

The surface appearance of the human gravesites needs to be considered separately, because these were not burrowed by animals. The human cadavers (and the calibration grave) were buried during summer periods in an area usually covered by grass, and Salvation Jane intermingled throughout, similar to the animal burial site vegetation. The observable signs of vegetation regrowth at the calibration site and human body graves were consistent with those recorded for the buried pigs and kangaroo areas. That is, after the graves were dug, the regrowth of vegetation followed the first winter rains. During the following summer period, growth became dry and died until the next winter rains. All plants growing on or near the gravesites were common to the area.

FIGURE 6.39
Human gravesite 1 (March 2002). Photograph faces south east.

FIGURE 6.40
From inside Human gravesite 1 cage (August 2002). Photograph faces south.

Figure 6.39 shows human gravesite 1 one month after burial, bereft of vegetation. It can be seen that the surrounding vegetation is dying off, being close to the end of summer.

Again, soursob and Salvation Jane were the first types of plants to begin growing on the upcast. These were lush and vigorous after the first winter (5.5 months after burial) over the gravesite 1 area (Figure 6.40). The large, leafy weeds in the centre of the photograph are the approximate position of where the head of the cadaver was laid. Note the soursob plants are taller at the outer rim of the direct grave area, towards the wire mesh areas.

As at the animal gravesites, a halo effect was observed in that no vegetation grew in areas where upcast had been placed and coincident with the grave areas themselves. This area of no vegetation was apparent in summer periods when vegetation died off and first appeared 12 months after burial (in the summer period). Figures 6.41–6.43 show the bare ground directly over and immediately around the gravesite compared with the grass in the field and to the edges of the cage.

The second human grave (grave 2) displayed a similar pattern as seen for the previous human grave in terms of vegetation regrowth (Figures 6.44 and 6.45). The water catchment basin created by piling earth around

FIGURE 6.41
Human gravesite 1 (December 2004). Photograph faces south.

FIGURE 6.42
Human gravesite 1 (December 2004). Photograph faces east.

FIGURE 6.43
Human gravesite 1 (October 2005). Photograph faces south.

FIGURE 6.44
Human gravesite 2 (December 2004). Photograph faces east.

FIGURE 6.45
Human gravesite 2 (October 2005). Photograph faces east.

the gravesite at grave 2 shows that this facilitated the growth of grass within the artificial basin. On the surrounding pile of upcast, it can be seen that there is very little vegetation, even of the hardy varieties.

The calibration pit demonstrated the same sequence of vegetation growth as for the two human graves. Small soursob plants grew over the grave, but more sparsely after it was created (during winter). Figure 6.46 shows the calibration pit the first winter after burial (6 months).

The calibration pit also demonstrated a halo area of no vegetation during the summer months, as shown in Figures 6.47 and 6.48. The ground is cracked and most of the vegetation is dead compared with the tufts around the area.

The calibration pit area was mown by the groundskeepers, as was the area surrounding human gravesites 1 and 2 (Figure 6.49).

Although there was only one calibration pit, the pattern of plant regrowth following ground disturbance suggests that the contents of a burial (a filled hole) do not strongly impact on the subsequent vegetation growth at the surface.

Consistent with the observations at the animal gravesites, it was again noticed there was no moss on any areas of upcast around the gravesites, although it was growing elsewhere in the field. As there were no trees near

FIGURE 6.46
Calibration pit (August 2003). Photograph faces east. The arrow points to the approximate centre of the pit.

FIGURE 6.47
Calibration pit (March 2004). (2 years after its creation). Photograph faces north.

FIGURE 6.48
Calibration pit (December 2004). Photograph faces north.

FIGURE 6.49
Calibration pit (October 2005). Photograph faces north.

to the gravesites, there was minimal ground debris (gumnuts or leaves) over the graves, but it was also relatively sparse over the surrounding area.

Soil (Upcast, Soil Resettling and Soil Colour)

Certain differences in the surface appearance of soil over an area may point to a potential gravesite. Where a grave is dug, areas with markedly contrasting soil horizons will mean that the different layers will be brought to the surface as upcast. Such soil may be of a different colour and/or texture to the surrounding surface soil. Conversely, where there are relatively indistinct soil horizons, the upcast may not contrast significantly to surface soil, although the texture may still be different. For example, upcast may contain rubble or small pebbles or other contrasting features. The upcast contrasted more at the animal gravesites than at the human gravesites with the surrounding soil due to the more distinctive soil horizons at the animal burial site.

At our observed gravesites, the soil related features that were of particular interest as these gravesites were monitored were: the endurance of differences in the colour of the upcast once exposed to weathering; extent of soil compaction and visible depressions; and signs of grave boundaries at the intersection of backfill with undisturbed soil (such as soil cracking).

The indicator most readily associated with gravesites is a mound of soil. Actually, the small resulting mounds when the graves were dug at some sites dissipated within a few short months after rains and were not enduring features. Immediately after burial, small mounds of upcast remained to one side of kangaroo sites 1 and 3. These mounds subsided and disappeared after 12 months (after the first winter season), presumably washed and spread out to some extent by rains. When the human burials were first dug, there were initial slight mounds of upcast near the gravesites, but these also disappeared within the first 6 months.

The area in which the kangaroos were buried had well-defined soil horizons, as shown in Figure 6.50. There was a lighter colour at the base, graduating to a rich red colour with the darker soil near the surface. It is the lighter colour and red soils that were brought to the surface as upcast, and the rubble textured upcast is seen at the right of the photograph.

Although there are slight variations in horizon spans, the soil profiles were fairly uniform at each of the burials. The typical soil profile for the kangaroo graves was:

0.15 m — Humus, brown, soft, rich.

0.25 m — Red compacted soil with charcoal.

0.30 m — Loam, light yellow (probably lumps of sandstone shale).

FIGURE 6.50
Kangaroo site 2 showing the differentiated soil horizons. Grave pit is shown looking north.

FIGURE 6.51
Pig grave soil profile (site 1).

FIGURE 6.52
Smithfield soil horizons as typified by human gravesite 2.

Although the pigs were buried in the same enclosure, the soil horizons in the actual burial area were not as well defined as the kangaroo graves, as can be seen in Figure 6.51. The soil type was red clay, of a fine to medium grain, and contained rubble that appeared as the hole reached approximately 0.5 m, at which there was a solid layer of limestone.

The soil at the human gravesite area was sandy at the surface, but became more clay with depth and, as stated earlier, in general the area was calcareous. The horizons are shown in Figure 6.52.

The colour of the upcast around the human gravesites was lighter than the surrounds and became richer with depth, although the contrast was not as great as at the animal gravesites (Figure 6.53). This is attributed to the less distinctive soil horizons seen at burial in this area.

The contrast of the upcast with the surrounding soil was an enduring indicator. For all animal graves, the upcast was apparent as a visual indicator for 5–6 years (pigs and kangaroo burials over the observation period respectively), and was distinguished by its colour and texture (containing rubble). Pig site 3 in Figure 6.54 shows the colour of the upcast that remained a lighter and pinker colour than the surface soil. During winter, the upcast soil was also distinctive if winter foliage was moved aside.

FIGURE 6.53
Calibration pit at its creation. It shows the contrast of the colour of the upcast.
Photograph faces north.

FIGURE 6.54
Pig site 3 at time of burial. The colour of the upcast clearly contrasts with the surface
soil. Photograph faces east.

In drier months, the soil around and directly overlying the graves (upcast) remained soft and powdery compared with the compacted hard soil in undisturbed areas, although the soil had the appearance of being cracked and hardened.

Soil resettling and the subsequent formation of a depression was observed at the first human body gravesite and the calibration site after 2 years. After 2.5 years, a small secondary depression was observed at human gravesite 1 and the calibration site. The artificial large mound surrounding the human gravesite 2 did not subside due to its size, although the soil settled over time. At this site the soil settled and a depression was observed, but it was difficult to determine if this was due to the collection of water in the middle of the catchment or if it was due to the fact there was a buried body present.

Did ground cover (leaves and twigs and such) have an effect on the upcast? Although the surface of the two animal sites located under the trees became covered in ground litter more quickly than the other graves, underneath the upcast had neither 'blended with the surrounds' nor changed colour. These sites were also less frequently disturbed by animals.

As might be expected, the animal scavenging at the unprotected animal graves obscured any signs of gradual depression formation that might have been attributed to the decomposition of remains. However, the human gravesites, protected from scavenging, showed depressions where the soil had resettled (including the calibration site). There was cracking and splitting of soil surfaces at the human gravesites, the calibration site and the animal gravesites around the edges of the gravesites (in unburrowed areas) coincident with the deposit of upcast at the surface, as has been noted by Duncan (1983).

Summary of Above Ground Changes to the Gravesites

Over several years, animal and human graves were observed for features at the grave surface that differentiated these areas from the surrounding landscape. The kangaroo graves were observed for a period of 6 years, the pig graves for 5 years and the two human gravesites for 3 and 2 years, respectively, according to when they were created during the research period. A sequence of surface changes was found to be common on all gravesites. These changes were moderated by the position of the grave within the landscape. Proximity to certain features of the landscape influenced the duration of the grave surface indicators and what may be termed the recovery of the gravesite appearance to that akin to its preburial state.

The surface features that differentiated the graves from their surroundings were: faunal scavenging at unprotected gravesites; an absence of ground litter (this took approximately 2 to 3 years to settle on the surface of the upcast) depending on the nearby landscape features; graves that were located in sheltered places became a repository for ground litter that masked other surface differences; enduring contrast of upcast; an absence of moss near the gravesites in wet periods; depressions formed at the human and calibration sites (unburrowed sites); and different patterns of vegetation growth during the drier or summer period, in particular, a necrotic zone. Plants that grew near or on the gravesites were typical of the preburial environment (regardless of season) and were restricted to low growing shallow-rooted plants.

The surfaces of the gravesites were transformed considerably because of the burrowing. This was the most dramatic and lasting surface change found at the nonprotected gravesites. After several years, as shown in this study, the burrows appeared as scooped out holes. The scavenging was not confined to any particular season.

The continued and intermittent burrowing and scavenging over several years has several implications. For example, such interference permanently changes any expected surface appearance of a grave. Clearly, digging and animal burrows can indicate the deposit of remains over several years. Further, the irregular soil disturbance will affect any vegetation regrowth, keeping the inner part of the grave free from much vegetation. Unearthed bones near the animal gravesites pointed to a nearby grave. The notable exceptions to recurrent burrowing were those graves at the bases of trees (kangaroo and pig sites 3). This was perplexing, but it is speculated as being related to the possible masking of odours by the ground litter or the other graves providing distractions. Perhaps if the only grave in the area was beneath a tree it still would have been scavenged. Scavenging would probably occur in most areas by some form of animal.

The unearthed soil was the primary factor impacting vegetation patterns rather than the presence of organic remains (human or animal) in the soil, as attested to by the regrowth patterns observed at the calibration pit. Shallow-rooted European weed types were the first plants to grow over the upcast, and these weeds were the most resilient plant types. At these gravesites, there was no sustained increase in the 'lushness' of the vegetation directly over the gravesites that is sometimes attributed to the presence of organic remains. The animal sites did show taller weed growth at interim intervals, but this was considered to be due to water catchment in the burrows.

In terms of visual indicators of graves provided by plant growth, there were distinct seasonal variations. Winter groundcover growth common to the area obscured the gravesites regardless of whether it was growing within the graves themselves. During the drier months, the upcast was found to have an inhibitory effect on vegetation due to its reduced capacity to retain water. Such areas I have termed 'halos' or 'necrotic zones'. These barren areas only occurred during summer and the interim seasons, and occurred soon after burial at all graves, coinciding approximately where upcast had been spread. As the calibration pit also had a barren area (halo), this does not suggest this phenomenon is due to the decomposition of either animals or humans in the graves. As the years progressed, this barren area did not remain as pronounced at all graves.

Depressions were not found at the animal gravesites because of the scavenging. However, depressions were found at one human gravesite and calibration pit after 2 years. After a further 6 months, there was a small secondary depression at both these sites. These depressions are attributed to the consolidation of the soil and its natural settling as a result of gravity (Rowell, 1994). When natural vegetation is present, soil does not consolidate, because it is in a state of equilibrium within the environment. It has its own structural stability and this serves to buffer it against natural forces (Rowell, 1994). The absence of vegetation during summer periods at the gravesites would have contributed to this process.

It was concluded from these results that the surface signs observed over 6 years were not affected by the variations in the contents of the graves or depth of the graves, to the extent that none were buried deeper than 1 m. The variations documented have been accounted for in terms of amount of shelter and positioning of the gravesites. The positioning of the animal burial under a tree shows that such gravesites in this type of location are not as readily visible in a search, because they are more likely to be covered by ground litter that shields any difference in upcast soil and may not be burrowed extensively. Both kangaroo site 3 and pig site 3, beneath trees, returned to their preburial states after 3 years, with the ground litter being thick after 2 years, except for the barely visible burrow. The implication of this finding is that any burial over 2 years old in an area with trees or shrubs for shelter may be expected to be masked by ground litter no matter what other surface signs are present beneath the ground litter.

The surface of all graves could be distinguished from the surrounding area through comparison of the upcast and associated soil cracking or surface softness with the surrounding soil, restricted vegetation growth in drier periods around the grave areas, especially summer, and burrowed holes (given access) directly over the graves. Any surface search for a grave would be easier if conducted during a drier month, as this would avoid the confounding effect of winter weed growth.

Aerial Surveillance: Surface Signs Observable From a Distance

Aerial surveillance was conducted over the animal graves to identify the observable signs of the gravesites from a distance. Given that the animal graves had been burrowed, it was expected that the disturbed holes would be seen from the air. Infrared film was used to survey the animal graves from a flying height of 1500 m AGL. The scale of the images was 1:10,000. The camera was a Wild RC30 230mm format using Kodak 2444 high resolution film.

Interestingly, no graves were visible from the resulting images obtained and this was attributed to three factors:

- height (too high for the necessary detail),
- existing ground cover and associated shadows obscured any potential signs of a grave, and
- angle of the camera (shadows masked and confounded ground variation).

Trees, shrubs and low-lying vegetation result in shadows that may easily obscure visible traces of a grave. Obviously, a highly cleared area would offer better results, but this is seldom the case in grave searches, and it is arguable that a clandestine grave would not usually be situated in a flat, cleared area.

Detection of a single gravesite using aerial surveillance in Australia is a high-risk source of information in that it should not be used as a sole source of data to state there is no grave in a search zone. Ordinarily in Australia, aerial surveillance for mapping purposes is at a height that does not allow for the detection of disturbances of the order of shallow graves. This is important information, because it means that photographic evidence of sites before burial would rarely be available to allow comparison of pre- and postburial situations, unless taken for a specific purpose at a lower height.

Subsurface Indications of Graves

The research graves were ideal sites on which to explore subsurface indicators of graves. Geophysical instruments offer such potential and have been used in investigations to locate graves with varied success, as was discussed in Chapter 2. Such instruments give information about the physical properties of an environment in a noninvasive way. The results of three instrument surveys are described here, as tested on the animal and human gravesites: ground penetrating radar (GPR), electromagnetic induction (EM) and direct current (DC) electrical resistivity.

Ground Penetrating Radar

Ground penetrating radar is used to detect changes in electromagnetic properties that are due to dielectric permittivity, conductivity and magnetic permeability. In applying GPR, an antenna transmitting electromagnetic waves in the subsurface is placed on the soil surface. A receiving antenna records reflected waves over the two-way time travel range. Electromagnetic properties are a function of subsurface material, structure, water content and bulk density. The recorded data produces reflecting interfaces as peaks of either negative or positive polarisation.

Three different types of GPR were used at the research graves. The equipment and postburial timing of each survey are stated in Table 6.5.

From these surveys it was found that soil disturbance is detected by the GPR. Associating the anomalies detected below the surface with organic remains is more difficult. In a search situation, it is not clear that these disturbances could be attributed to the buried remains any more than other objects beneath the surface, such as clothing items.

The first example described took place at the kangaroo grave area. Ground penetrating radar was used to survey kangaroo sites 1 and 3 on the day of burial (March 1999). A SPR Scan (from ERA Technology) using a 500 MHz antenna mounted on a low-lying trolley with wheels for manoeuvrability (see Figure 6.55) was wheeled across the greater length of the two graves. Kangaroo site 1 was in the open area and site 3 was located near the base of a tree. Kangaroo site 2 was not surveyed, because the logs near the grave impeded the movement of the GPR trolley.

TABLE 6.5
Ground Penetrating Radar Survey Dates

Date of survey	GPR type	Gravesites tested	Length of time after burial
Survey 1 March 1999	SPR Scan (ERA Technology)	Kangaroo sites 1 and 3	On day of burial
Survey 2 January 2001	PulseEKKO 100 system (Sensors and Software version 1.2)	Kangaroo sites 1,2,3. Pig sites 1,2,3	22 months. 6 months.
Survey 3 January 2004	RAMAC GPR 500 MHz	Human grave 1, Calibration pit	23 months 11 months

At the time of the survey, the soil in the area was dry and hard, as it was near the end of the summer period. The graves had just been dug and therefore the soil was overturned and disturbed, and had not resettled.

The survey results showed indications of soil disturbance coincident with the position of the two graves (kangaroo sites 1 and 3), on the day of interment. The result for kangaroo site 1 is shown below (Figure 6.56).

Given the solid frozen state of the kangaroos at the time of the survey, it was expected that the indicators might have been more definitive. Using more than one antenna may also produce better determinations of subsurface disturbance.

The kangaroo graves were surveyed again when they had been buried for 2 years (January 2001). The ground was dry (as this was the summer period). The GPR applied in this survey was a PulseEKKO 100 system (Sensors and Software version 1.2). A 200MHz antenna was selected, which allowed a penetration depth at this frequency of approximately 4 m and a resolution of approximately 5 cm. The GPR had a ground coupled dipole antennae, 100-Volt transmitter, receiver and a laptop computer for logging data collected onsite (facilitating real-time display). To use this GPR, the transmitting and receiving antennae are stepped along in small increments (between 0.2 and 0.5 m), while maintaining a constant separation. Data processing was undertaken using PulseEKKO software (version 1.2). The equipment is shown in Figure 6.57.

The orientation survey showed the near surface as flat-lying with uniform strata, reflecting *in situ* soils developed on bedrock. The signal seemed to be almost completely attenuated below approximately 1 m depth (probably due to the high-clay soils in the area).

The GPR produced anomalies that could be equated with the depth and position of the three kangaroo graves, and expected associated disturbance. The known three kangaroo graves were located at approximately the 4-m survey length mark in Figures 6.58–6.60. Kangaroo site 1 appears to be identifiable in Figure 6.58 almost 2 years after burial.

The kangaroo was buried at a depth of 1 m and this survey line was lengthwise. There are two large objects shown in the survey results along the length of the grave and it cannot be determined whether these are reflections from bone or clothing items.

Disturbance is also featured in the results for kangaroo site 2, including reflections of more solid features that could be bones from the kangaroo or items of clothing. However, there is not a singular feature in this survey that can be definitely equated with the kangaroo.

FIGURE 6.55
The ERA technology ground penetrating radar. This was used for the surveys at the time of kangaroo burials. Note the trolley application. Photograph faces south.

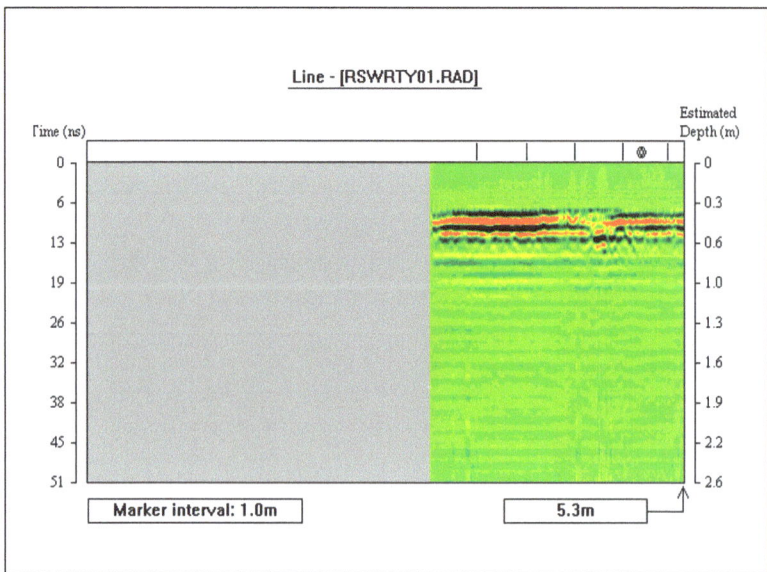

FIGURE 6.56
Kangaroo site 1 (lateral across filled grave).

FIGURE 6.57
GPR PulseEKKO 100 system.

The disturbance is shown on the survey results for kangaroo site 3 (Figure 6.60), even though this was taken across the width of the grave. Although there is disturbance, the features are not distinct as were those of kangaroo site 1. Kangaroo site 3 was positioned near the base of a tree and this may have obscured the GPR results.

The pig graves were surveyed using the same GPR as for the kangaroo graves when they had been buried for 6 months (January 2001). Scavengers (foxes) had extensively burrowed each of the graves. Strong reflections coincident with and overlapping the grave were found, compared with relatively weak signals on either side of the grave. Figures 6.61–6.66 show the results for the three pig grave surveys. The first figure for pig site 1 (Figure 6.61) is the line across the narrowest part of the burrowing.

Pig site 2 (buried near small bushes) also showed disturbances coincident with the grave. Two traverses of the GPR at right angles to each other were taken and are shown in Figures 6.62 (lengthwise) and 6.63 (across the width) for pig site 2. The disturbance showing on both lines was at a depth of 0.43 m, at which the pig was buried.

At pig site 3, strong reflections coincident with and overlapping the grave were found, compared with relatively weak signals coincident with either side of the grave. These anomalous readings could be the detection

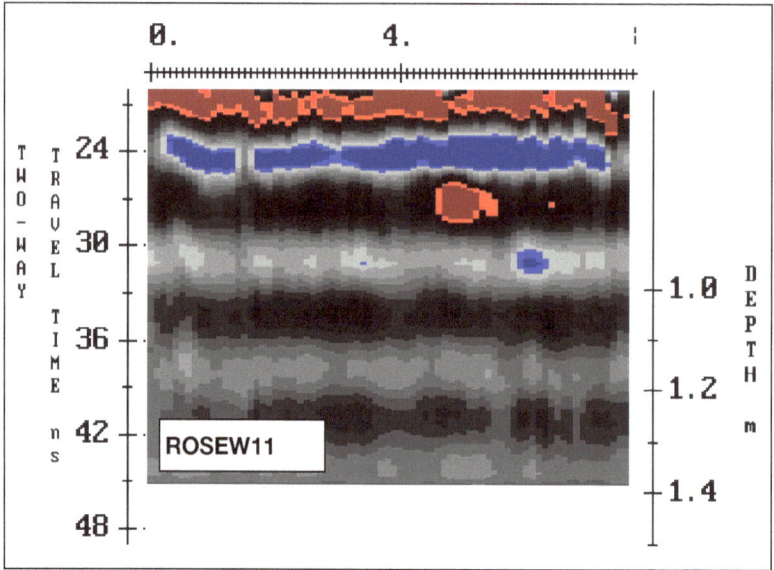

FIGURE 6.58

GPR survey for kangaroo site 1. A kangaroo grave shown using GPR at 1.0 m depth. The grave contained cotton and woollen clothing, including a metal belt buckle. Survey was taken across the length of the grave.

of the carcass, disruption of a soil or clay layer, or from reverberations within the excavation. It is also possible that nearby tree roots could have been influencing the results.

The survey line results shown in Figure 6.65 were from along the eastern edge of the burrowing. The circled object could be the remains of tree roots. It is, however, coincident with the depth of burial.

Figure 6.66 shows disturbance and scattered anomalies. It is not clear what these might be, but from the position of the survey line they do not coincide with the position of the buried pig. The reflections demonstrate that anomalies coincident with the buried animals do not differ in signature from the reflections coincident with other objects, such as rocks, tree roots or clumps of different soil types.

There are differences in the results of the kangaroo burials compared with the pig burials. Differences between the burials that were expected to impact on the capacity for grave detection by GPR (and subsequent results) were the size of the animals (kangaroos have larger carcasses with larger bones), effect of burrowing (as this was more marked over the pig burials) and duration of burial (there may have been more soil settling at

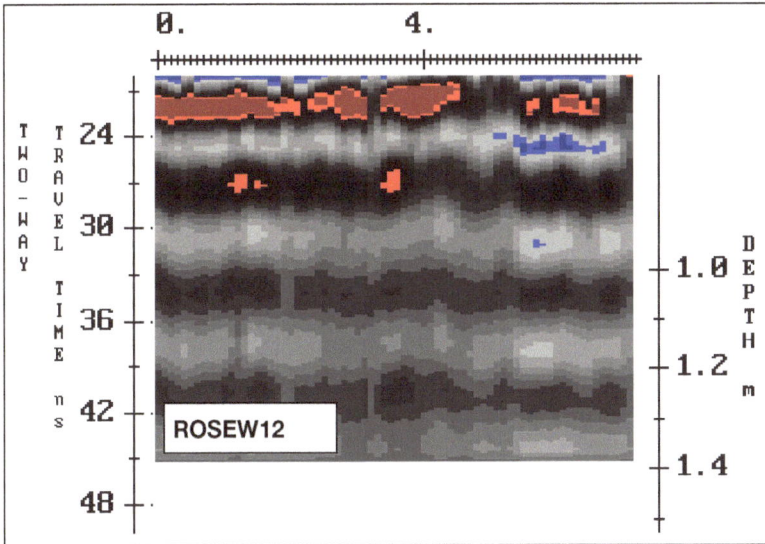

FIGURE 6.59
GPR survey for kangaroo site 2. This reading shows disturbance but the features are not as clearly distinguishable. The grave is at approximately 0.75m depth. The grave contained cotton and synthetic clothing, including a belt buckle. The survey was taken across the length of the grave.

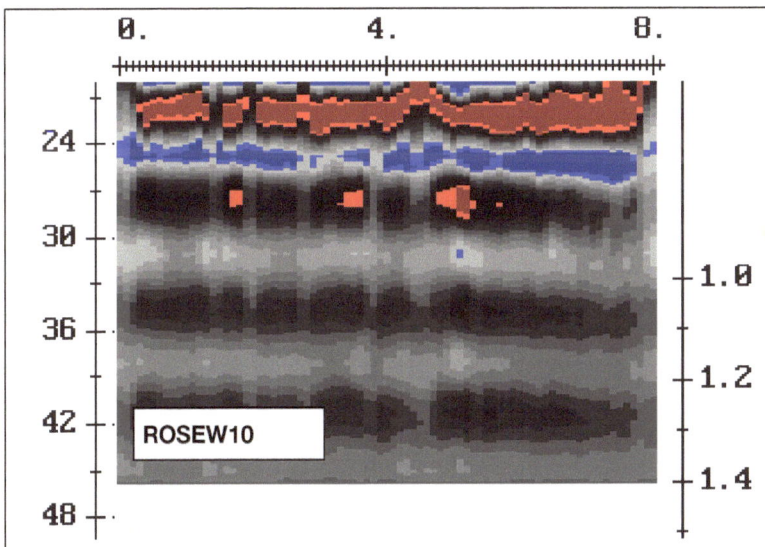

FIGURE 6.60
GPR survey for kangaroo site 3. The traverse line passed over the centre of the burrowing at the 4 m mark at approximately 0.59 m depth across the width of the grave. This kangaroo was covered in a plastic bag in addition to cotton and synthetic clothing.

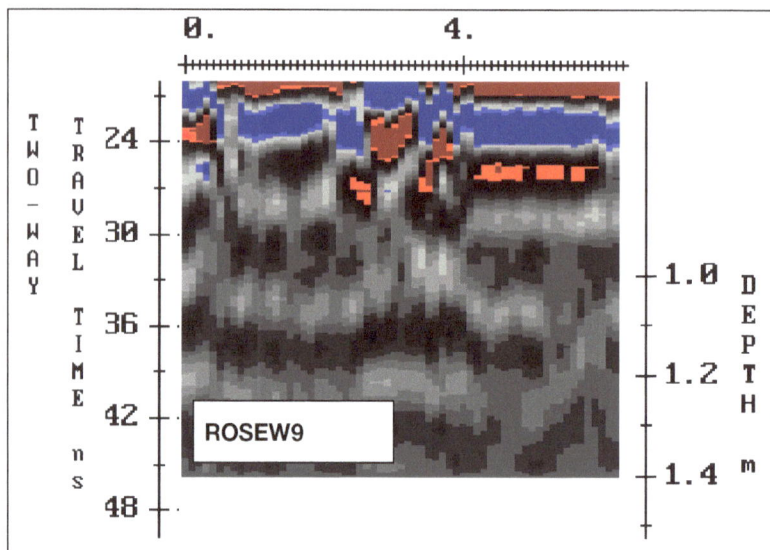

FIGURE 6.61
GPR survey for pig site 1. This pig grave is clearly depicted (using GPR) 6 months after burial at a depth of 0.5 m. The pig was buried in a plastic garbage bag, left unsealed. The survey was taken across the width of the grave.

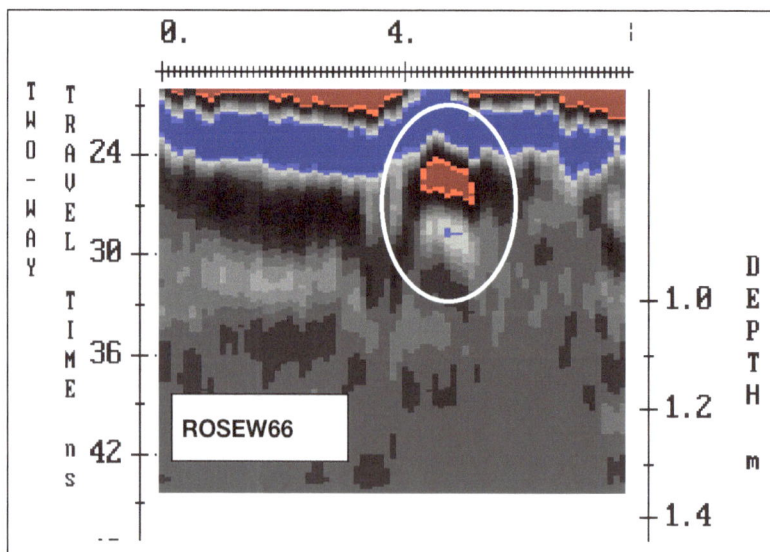

FIGURE 6.62
GPR survey for pig site 2. Pig 2 is clearly depicted (using GPR) 6 months after burial at 0.43 m. The pig was clothed in cotton and synthetic items, including a metal belt buckle and rubber-soled sandshoes. The survey was taken along the length of the grave.

the older kangaroo burials). The kangaroos were buried deeper (with no kangaroo being above 0.59 m) compared with the more shallow buried pigs (the deepest being 0.5 m). The faunal burrowing was apparent from the surface disturbance at each site. The greater disturbance shown in the pig surveys equates with the significant amount of burrowing over the pig burials. It may be that the disturbances and anomalies able to be detected by the GPR are likely to be more pronounced the more recent the burial. Schultz et al. (2002) made this suggestion based on similar results in pigs buried and surveyed using GPR over a 21-month period. The reasons for this may be related to length of burial, suggesting that GPR is more sensitive to recent soil disturbances, or perhaps the remains themselves including clothing items (it is presumed without excavation that the kangaroos had undergone a greater degree of decomposition than the pigs at this time of burial duration). It is unlikely the pigs were skeletonised after only a few months.

Ground Penetrating Radar Survey — Human Gravesite 1 and Calibration Pit

Human gravesite 1 and the calibration pit were surveyed using GPR when the human body had been buried for almost 2 years (23 months) and the calibration pit had been created almost 1 year previously (11 months), in January 2004. The GPR was a RAMAC GPR 500MHz with X3M console (developed by Malå GeoScience of Sweden). Survey lines were traversed at intervals of 0.5 m across the length and width of human gravesite 1 (five lines across the length and five lines across the width comprising 30 m) in east–west and north–south directions. Reflections from the wire mesh cage surrounding human gravesite 1 resulted in signal interference, but these effects were removed through data processing.

For all profiles, a trace was collected at each 0.02-m interval along survey lines, as determined by a calibrated survey wheel attached to the radar system. Throughout the acquisition, signal stacking was used, with the compromise between survey speed and data quality found to be optimal at eight stacks per measurement. This means that each recorded trace (0.02 m) is the mean response from eight individual radar pulses. The total time window of 30 ns was collected and 250 samples were recorded in this time period. Therefore, each sample represents approximately 0.12 ns of the record. Assuming mean substrate velocity of 0.1 m/ns, this equates to a sample interval of 0.005 m.

The centre frequency of the antenna applied was 500 MHz (5×10^8 cycles per second). The dimension of the complete wavelength of this

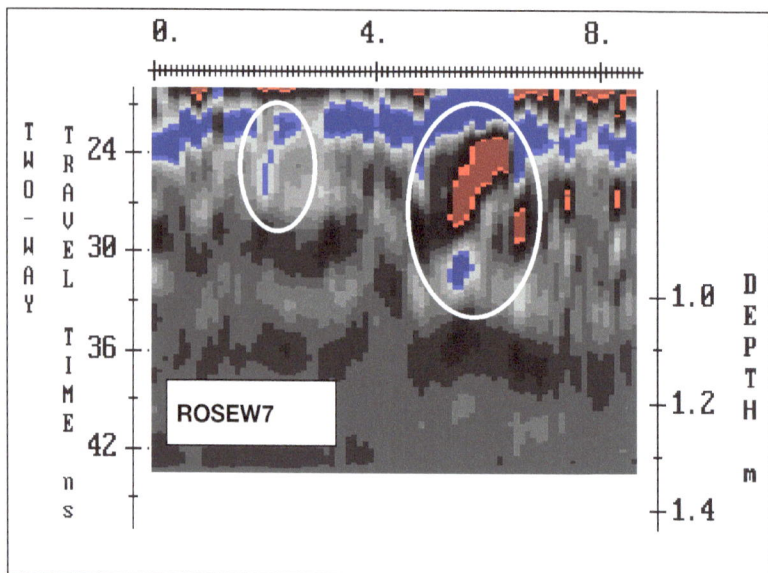

FIGURE 6.63
GPR survey for pig site 2. This survey was taken across the width of the grave.

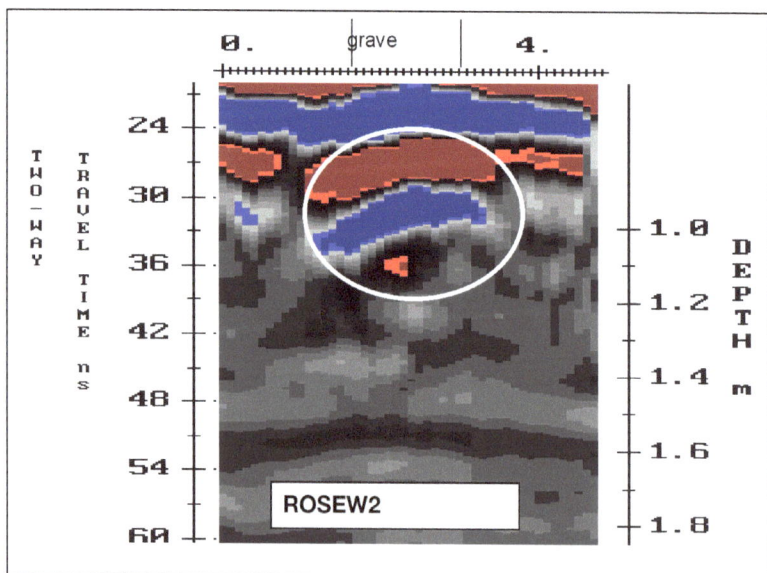

FIGURE 6.64
GPR survey for pig site 3. Pig 3 is clearly identified (using ground penetrating radar) 6 months after burial at 0.5m. The pig was buried in cotton clothing only. The survey was taken along the length of the grave.

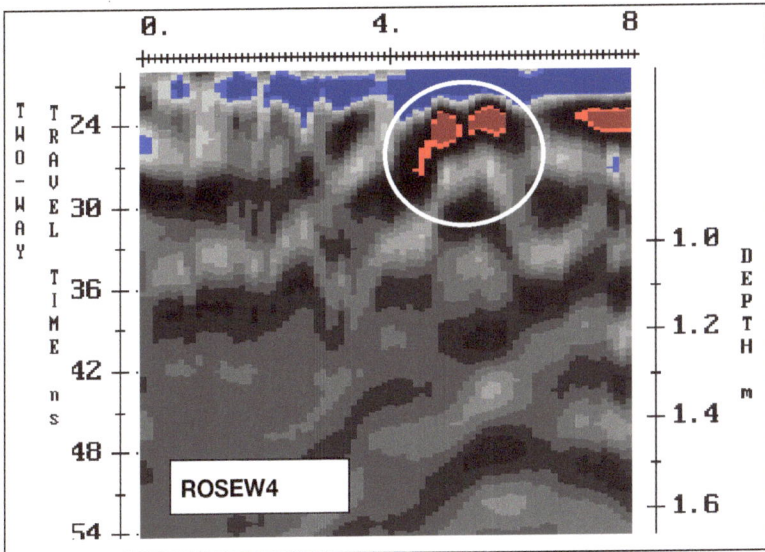

FIGURE 6.65
GPR survey for pig site 3. This survey line was taken on the edge of the grave across the far width of the burrowing (at the eastern end).

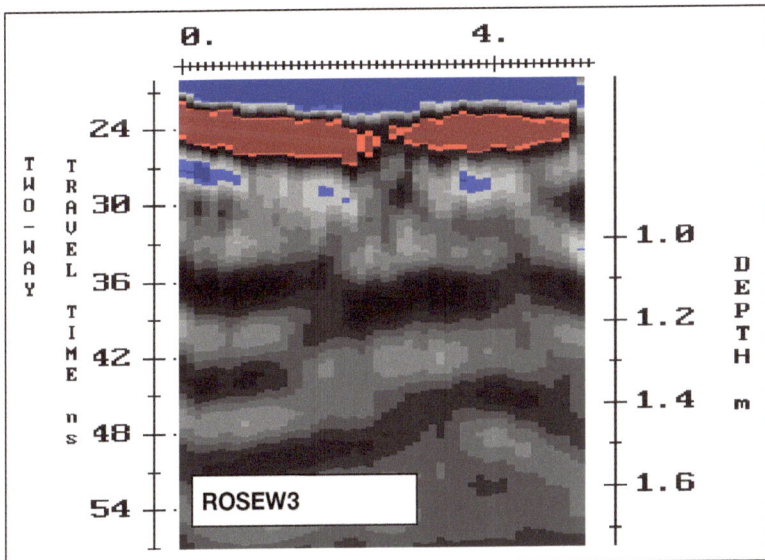

FIGURE 6.66
GPR survey for pig site 3. This survey line was taken at the southern edge of the burrowing (not over the centre of the grave) along the length. It was approximately 1 m from the centre of the burrowing.

signal in a material with a dielectric constant equal to 9 (pulse velocity = 0.1 m/ns) is estimated to be 0.22 m. The vertical resolution is considered equal to the thinnest horizontal structure capable of producing a reflection of the incident signal in a medium. Under these conditions, the vertical resolution of this survey is 0.055 m = ¼ of the wavelength.

The data quality was considered good. However, the uniformity of the surface soil and the likely high clay content at the burial area suggested featureless data away from the gravesites. There was an attenuating effect of surrounding materials.

The human gravesite survey results suggest detection of human remains, although the signature was not distinct in shape and had been interpreted as such because of the known body within the grave. The human grave was situated at survey lines 2, 3 and 4 in Figure 6.67 and this was where the anomalies were identified. The responses at these profiles showed strong irregular reflectors at a shallow depth coincident with the refilled grave above the body. It was only the north–south profiles that were considered anomalous compared with the calibration pit. The east–west profiles did not show significant reflectors above the known body.

The reflectors in survey lines 2, 3 and 4 were calculated as occurring at a depth of between 0.55 and 0.1 m (assuming a substrate velocity of 0.1 m/ns). There was also a faint horizontal reflector between 0.7 and 0.8 m BGS, which could be identified as the grave bottom. At the depth where the body lay (0.75 m), the responses were weak and there are no significant reflectors. There was a zone of attenuation coincident with the body. The high amplitude reflections that occurred in the soil above the known body were attributed to the disturbance of soil.

By way of comparison, Figure 6.68 shows the GPR results for the calibration pit (located at survey lines 3, 4 and 5). There were some weak reflections that occurred from the surface to deep (late) in the radar record and appeared to define the edges of the grave (approximately 1 m across).

From 0.6 m, the reflectors were thicker and extended beyond the width of the known grave dimensions. These could be artifacts in the data as a result of strong reflecting surfaces within the grave or alternatively the disturbed earth may have allowed preferential infiltration of water so that there were localised changes in soil moisture levels. Water would significantly influence the radar response from the subsurface. It is also noted that at 0.8 m along the profile for survey line 8, there was an anomaly suspected to be a small metallic object.

The results show that the GPR is most likely to demonstrate disturbed soil rather than the body itself.

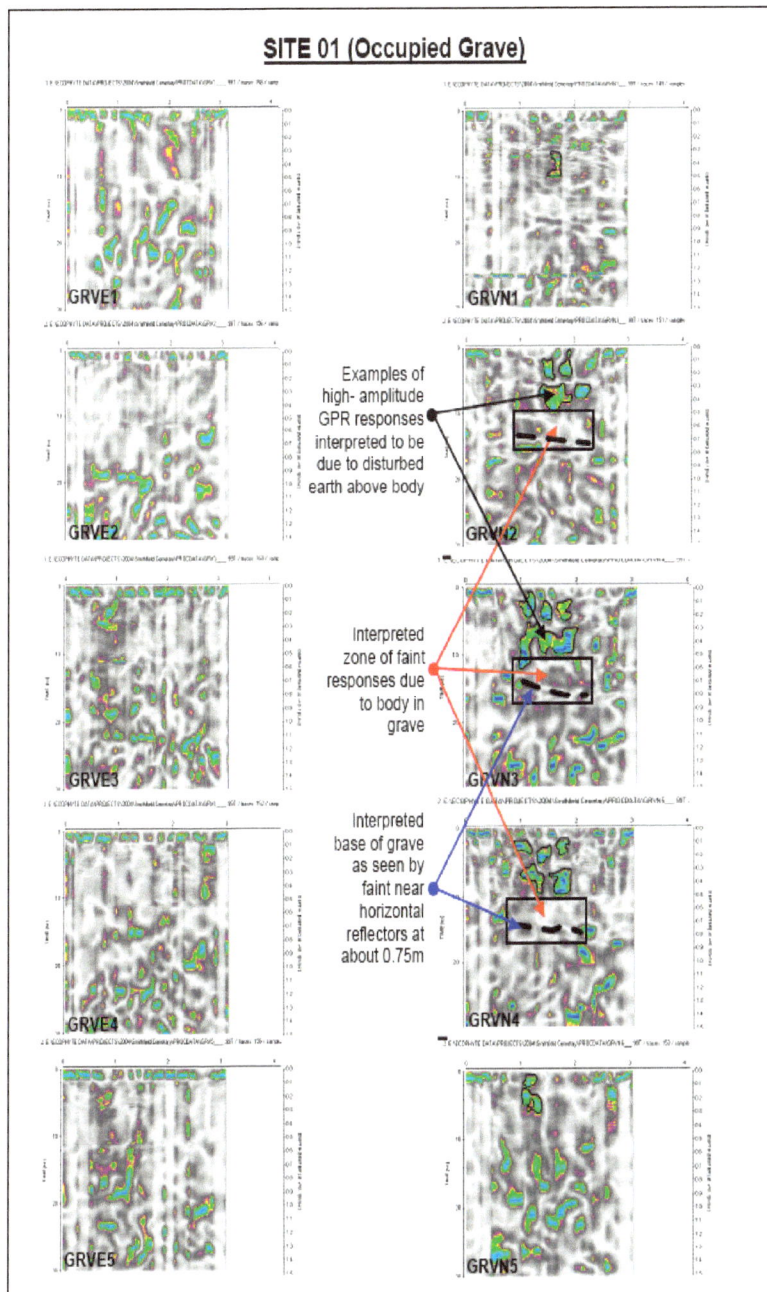

FIGURE 6.67
Ground penetrating radar results for human gravesite 1.

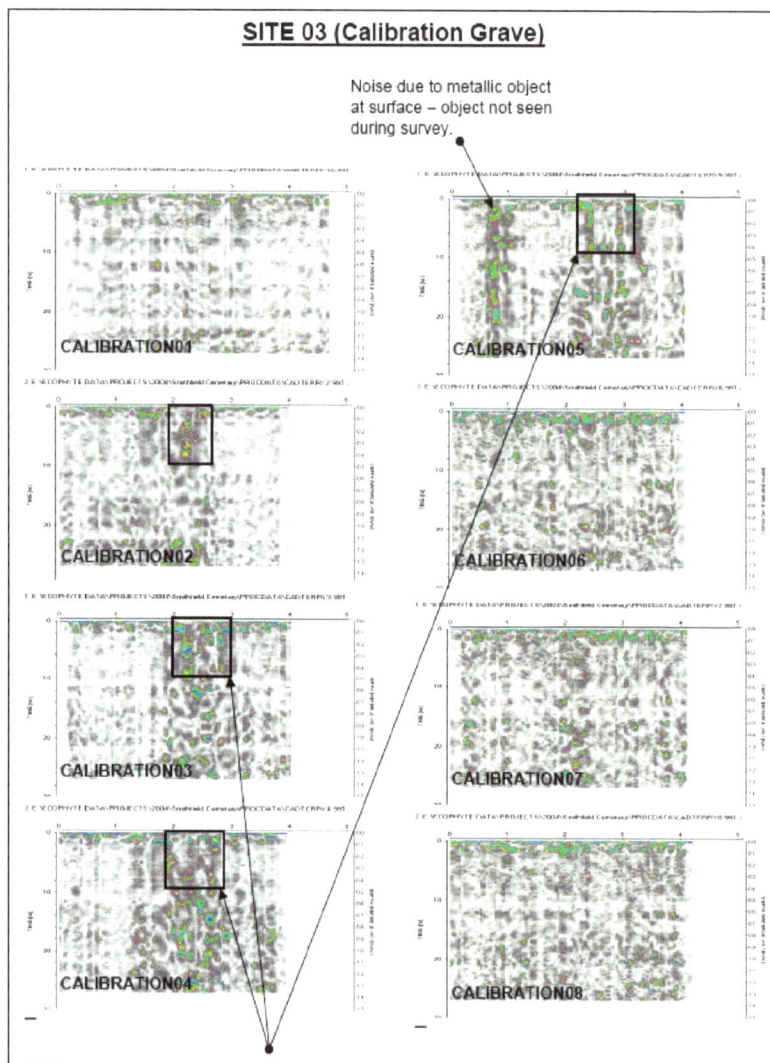

FIGURE 6.68
Ground penetrating radar results for calibration pit.

Electrical Resistivity Surveys

In an electrical resistivity survey, the resistance to an electric current by soil and other anomalies is measured and used as a basis for determining variations across an area. Although this is a rarely used method for forensic gravesite detections, there is a logical basis for expecting that this type of survey could prove successful under suitable conditions. Resistivity surveying is dependent on several factors: the porosity of the soil and the chemical content of the water within the pore spaces (Hole & Heizer, 1965; Killam, 1990), soil type, degree of saturation, temperature of pore water and the concentration of ions (Yoon & Park, 2001). Salts from the soil and biological humics determine the ionic concentration of soil, which affect conductivity (Killam, 1990). Partially saline water also lowers resistance (Killam, 1990). It is likely a grave area would have a higher moisture content and a higher level of organic matter, increased concentrations of ionised water and therefore a lower resistivity (Killam, 1990; Owsley, 1995).

Electrical resistivity surveys were carried out over the kangaroo and human gravesites, and the calibration pit. Included in this section is the application of electrical resistivity to the detection of a historical burial in an outer South Australian township that was approximately 150 years old.

This survey technique involves placing electrodes in the ground at regular intervals and sending an electric current through one of them. The resistance to an electric current by soil and other anomalies is measured as the ratio of voltage across the electrodes to the current flowing through them. Anomalously high or low resistivity scores form the basis for detecting features and anthropic soil horizons (McManamon, 1984).

The results of three separate are presented in this section (Table 6.6).

Direct current (DC) resistivity was used to survey two kangaroo sites (1 and 2) when the kangaroos had been buried for 22 months. Twelve electrodes were spaced at 0.2 m intervals along the length of the graves. The applied current was 5 mA. At kangaroo site 1, readings were taken from a line that ran north–south. At kangaroo site 2, the line was in an east–west direction (this was because of the nearby logs obstructing the readings). The tree logs are shown in Figure 6.69.

TABLE 6.6
Dates of Electrical Resistivity Surveys

Date of survey	Electrical resistivity instrument type	Gravesites tested	Length of time since burial
January 2001	Direct current resistivity	Kangaroo sites 1 and 2	22 months
April 2004	STING	Human grave 1, human grave 2 and calibration pit	2 years 1 month 1 year 3 months
2001	STING	Historical human gravesite	150 years

FIGURE 6.69
Resistivity survey line over kangaroo site 2 (east–west survey line).

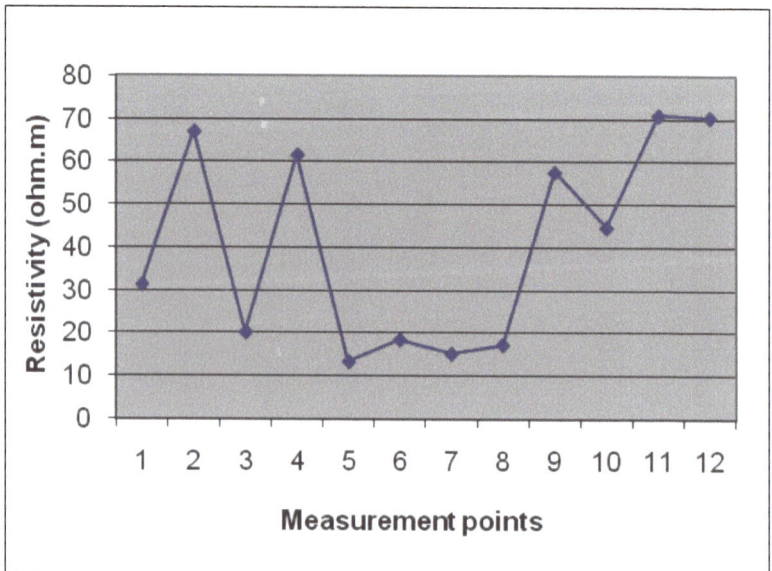

FIGURE 6.70
Kangaroo site 1 resistivity profile (north–south).

The weather was hot and dry (being January, the summer period) and the ground surface was dry and hardened. However, despite these conditions the two kangaroo graves demonstrated lower resistivity levels coincident with the location of the graves. In Table 6.7, the bold type highlights the lower resistivity readings obtained at the measurement positions that relate to the burial of kangaroo site 1 (measurement positions 5–8).

This survey line went over the width of the grave and therefore there are just four measurement positions with a lower resistivity reading compared with a lengthwise survey line. This lower resistivity coincident with the kangaroo burial is shown graphically in Figure 6.70.

Similar results were obtained at kangaroo site 2, at which lower resistivity levels were found at measurement positions 3–8 that coincided with the location of the kangaroo burial (highlighted in Table 6.8). This survey line went over the length of the grave. The area of lower resistivity is shown in Figure 6.71.

Lower resistivity measures were obtained coincident with kangaroo burials 1 and 2 compared with the adjacent non-grave areas. These results suggest higher water retention in these zones, perhaps trapped in remnants of the clothing within the graves. The results at kangaroo site 1 are consistent with the higher conductivity results obtained at kangaroo site 1 discussed later.

An electrical resistivity survey was carried out over the two human graves and the calibration pit when the human body at gravesite 1 had been buried for two years, the human body at human gravesite 2 for one

TABLE 6.7
Kangaroo Site 1 Resistivity Results

Electrode measurement position	Position (array midpoint) (m)	Measured voltage (mV)	Apparent resistivity (ohm.m)
1	0.3	125.0	31.4
2	0.5	267.0	67.1
3	0.7	80.5	20.2
4	0.9	245.0	61.6
5	1.1	53.5	**13.4**
6	1.3	73.6	**18.5**
7	1.5	60.6	**15.2**
8	1.7	69.0	**17.3**
9	1.9	229.0	57.6
10	2.1	178.0	44.7
11	2.3	282.0	70.9
12	2.5	280.0	70.4

TABLE 6.8
Kangaroo Site 2 Resistivity Results

Electrode measurement position	Position (array midpoint) (m)	Measured voltage (mV)	Apparent resistivity (ohm.m)
1	0.3	665.0	167.1
2	0.5	492.0	123.7
3	0.7	113.0	**28.4**
4	0.9	30.9	**7.8**
5	1.1	79.3	**19.9**
6	1.3	30.5	**7.7**
7	1.5	51.4	**12.9**
8	1.7	166.0	**41.7**
9	1.9	663.0	166.6
10	2.1	363.0	91.2
11	2.3	725.0	182.2

month, and the calibration pit had been in place for 1 year and 3 months. On the day of the survey, the weather was overcast and mild (19°C), but conditions had been hot the previous week. Consequently, the surface soil was damp, but dry underneath.

STING electrical resistivity equipment was used in a Wenner Array resistivity arrangement, because it is most sensitive to near-surface changes in resistivity (Killam, 1990). A continuous profiling technique (in which spacing between electrodes is kept constant) was used and four electrodes were used (two electrodes conducted current and two electrodes were for voltage). Figure 6.72 shows the position of the caged human gravesites surveyed and gives compass directions.

There were four survey lines (running east–west) using 20 points at 1 m intervals. These lines were repeated four times (increasing the separation to a = 2, 3 and 4 m progressively). The larger the separation, the greater the penetration of current and hence the deeper the readings were considered more likely to provide data about the subsurface. The position of the graves or pit was between 9.5 m and 10.5 m points. The data (see Figure 6.73) were modelled using the program *Res2Dinv*.

The orientation survey shows a uniform subsurface structure and indicates dry, air-filled soils grading to water-filled soils at 2 m depth. The lowest plot in Figure 6.73 is the smooth resistivity model, generated by inversion of the observations in the top profile.

The results of the calibration pit (shown in Figure 6.74) are similar to the orientation survey (Figure 6.73), but there is a slightly lower resistivity at the

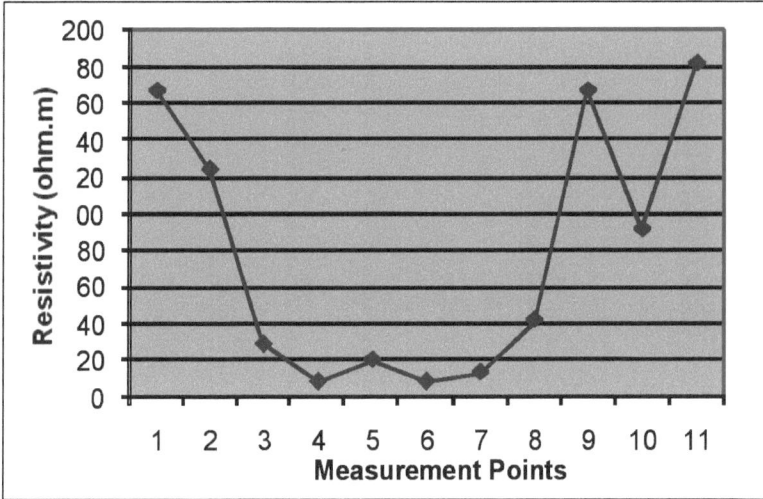

FIGURE 6.71
Kangaroos site 2 resistivity profile (east–west).

9 m position by a factor of 2 that indicates a change in porosity (of a factor of approximately 1.4).

The results of the resistivity survey over human gravesite 1 (Figure 6.75) indicate a very resistive zone coincident with the gravesite. It is likely this is because the soil had no vegetation cover and was much drier.

The results of the resistivity survey over human gravesite 2 show little variation (Figure 6.76), although there is higher resistivity over the area of the gravesite compared with adjacent areas. This burial was only 1 month old.

The higher resistivity readings over the gravesites compared with the surrounding areas may reflect the high evaporation rates where there is no vegetation and there is less moisture retention. This was more apparent at human gravesite 1 than either the calibration pit or human gravesite 2. It is possible this is related to soil settling over time and the resulting differences in soil porosity. Resistivity contrast depends on the difference in soluble ion concentration, as well as the mobility of the ions in the soil

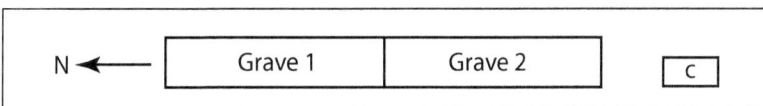

FIGURE 6.72
Orientation of human graves in relation to compass directions.
Note: 'C' indicates the position of the calibration pit.

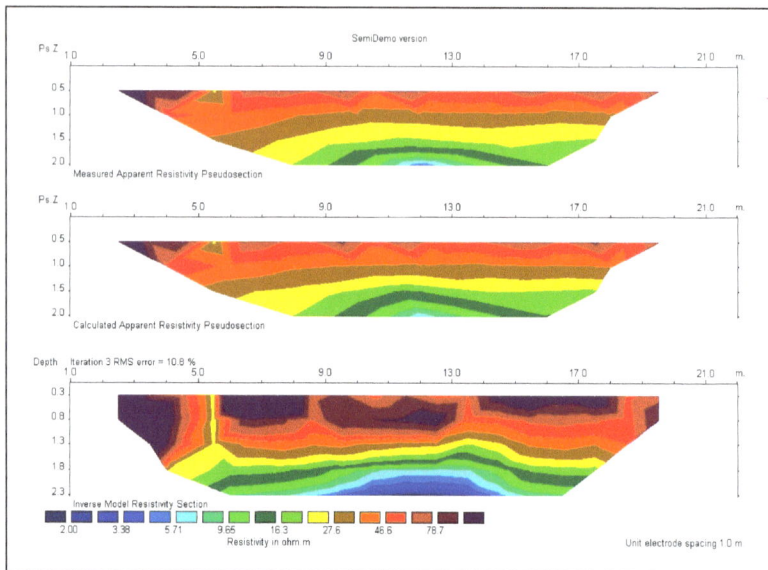

FIGURE 6.73
Orientation survey (electrical resistivity).

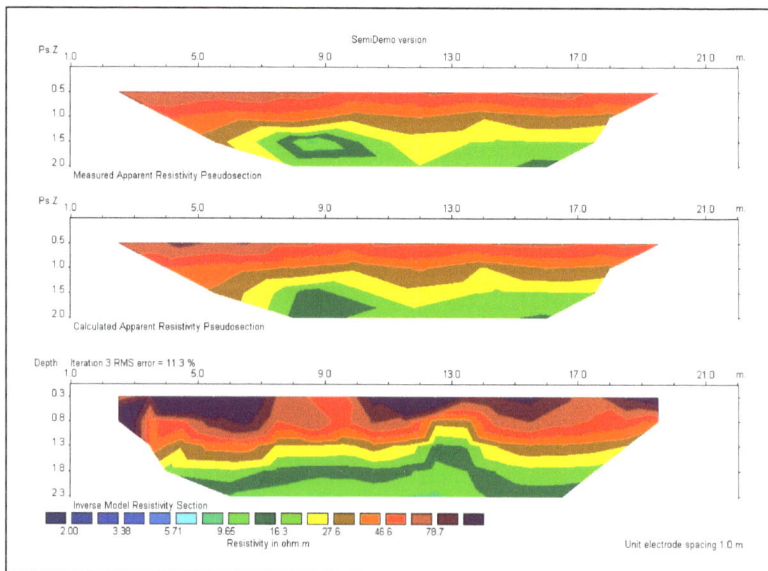

FIGURE 6.74
Electrical resistivity results for calibration pit.

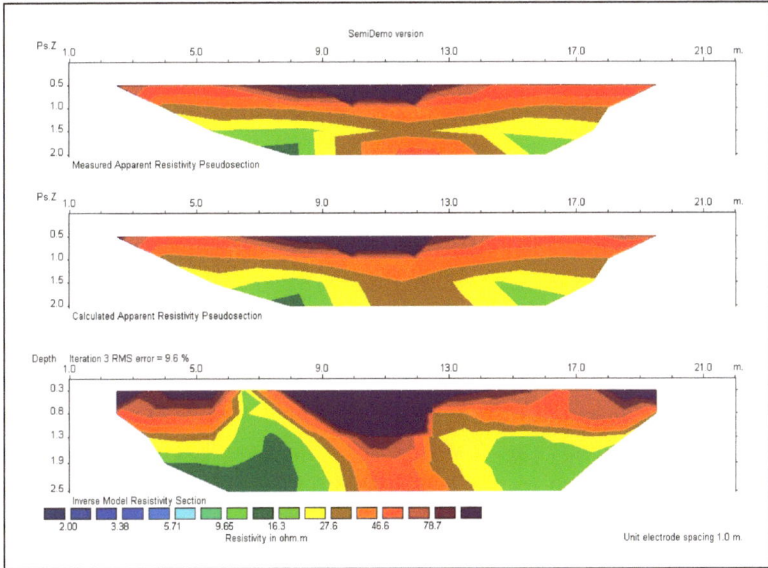

FIGURE 6.75
Electrical resistivity results for human grave 1.

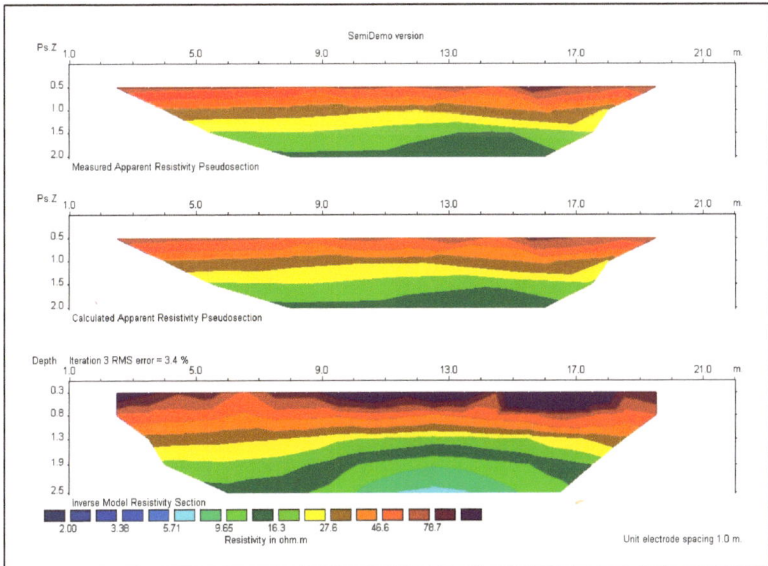

FIGURE 6.76
Electrical resistivity results for human grave 2.

and the shaft. Soluble ions require soluble salts and water both to be present (these depend on soil type, consolidation and precipitation). In these surveys, the dry soil has impacted on the resistivity results. As a technique, resistivity is more effectively used in less extreme months because of its reliance on soil moisture levels (David and Linford, 2000).

Electrical Resistivity Survey of a Historical Burial

A locally owned field in Willunga (small coastal township), South Australia, was thought to contain a burial that had occurred some 150 years earlier. This had been a formal burial of a landowner on what had been his own property, most likely in a coffin. Local residents had asked that the burial be located.

The soil type in the area is classified as alluvial. The area was cleared of plants and trees, and only low-lying grass was growing on the flat plain area, bordered by fences. Any potential surface indicators were obscured by cultivation of the land since the burial, especially the topsoil of the field that had been heavily excavated and ploughed for the past 50 years.

Electrical resistivity (a STING system) was used to survey several key areas in the field. Twenty electrodes were placed in a Wenner Array pattern, spaced at 0.5 m intervals along a straight line at several locations across the field (Figure 6.77).

An area of lower resistivity was identified and it was here that the burial was found and excavated (Figure 6.78). It had been anticipated that areas of lower resistivity might be indicative of areas in which moisture had collected owing to the grave and coffin.

Subsequent excavation revealed the grave, beginning with the coffin that was coincident with the site of lower resistivity. A backhoe was used to scrape the top layers of soil. The soil had clearly been disturbed as it was of a mixed colouring and there were no clearly defined horizons. The timber coffin was 1.5 m below the surface, and crumbled as it was handled. Clay had seeped into the coffin and there were no voids (air pockets) inside. The coffin contained human skeletal remains embedded in clay. Fine plant roots were growing throughout the skeleton and were attached to all the bones.

Electrical resistivity was successful in detecting human remains buried in a coffin, with the key indicator being lower electrical resistivity relative to the surrounding area. The presence of the coffin was most likely a major contributing factor to the grave's detection by electrical resistivity because of its capacity to hold clay and water, and the possible retention of dissolved conductive ions. The value of the geophysical instrument was

FIGURE 6.77
The STING electrical resistivity equipment. Wenner-Array pattern used over various areas of the field.

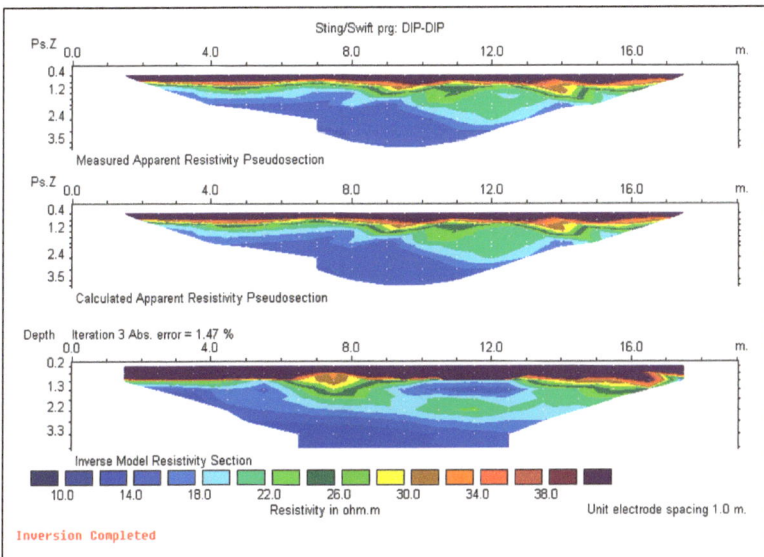

FIGURE 6.78
Results of electrical resistivity at Willunga. This includes the inversion model (bottom diagram). Note the shallow low-resistivity anomaly between 11 and 12 m along the profile.

its capacity to detect contrast; the survey did not detect the body itself but secondary factors relating to the physical nature of gravesites.

Electromagnetic Surveys

Electromagnetic (EM) induction meters induce an electromagnetic current into the ground, providing a means of measuring the electrical conductivity of subsurface features (Davenport, 2001). In terms of clandestine graves, disturbed ground may have a different conductivity to undisturbed ground (Davenport, 2001). The electrical conductivity of soil increases as the water, clay or metal content increases and as the concentration of dissolved ions increases in water (Fischer, 1980; Nobes, 2000). The purpose of the surveys discussed in this section was to determine whether differences in conductivity over the gravesites were consistent enough to link any anomalous readings to the known gravesites. The two surveys carried out over the animal and human gravesites were both carried out during summer periods at which time the ground surfaces were relatively dry (Table 6.9).

Electromagnetic Survey 1

Electromagnetic surveys using a Geonics EM31-D terrain conductivity meter were carried out over one kangaroo grave (site 1) and one pig grave (site 2) in January 2001. The kangaroo had been buried for 22 months and the pig for 6 months. The Geonics EM31-D terrain conductivity meter was used in quadrature (bulk conductivity) mode with measurements made for two orientations of the coil. Vertical and horizontal readings were taken on survey lines across the length of both kangaroo site 1 and pig site 2. The survey line length was 30 m for each grave, with the graves being approximately at the midpoint.

TABLE 6.9
Electromagnetic Survey Dates

Date of survey	GPR type	Gravesite tested	Length of time since burial
Survey 1 January 2001	Geonics EM31-D terrain conductivity meter	Kangaroo site 1, pig site 2	22 months 6 months
Survey 2 December 2003	EM38 electromagnetic induction meter	Kangaroos sites 1, 2, 3; Pig sites 1, 2, 3; Human grave 1; Calibration pit	4 years 9 months 3 years 5 months 1 year 10 months 11 months

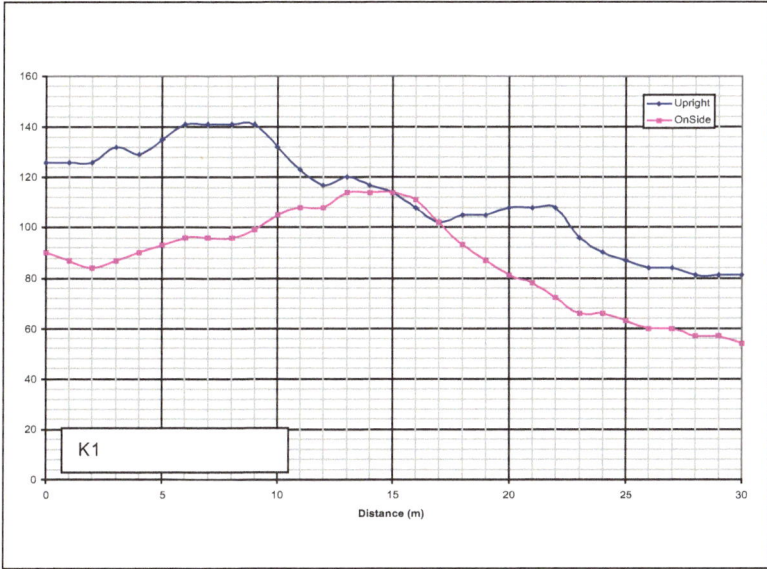

FIGURE 6.79
Kangaroo site 1 EM results. Vertical and horizontal readings are shown.

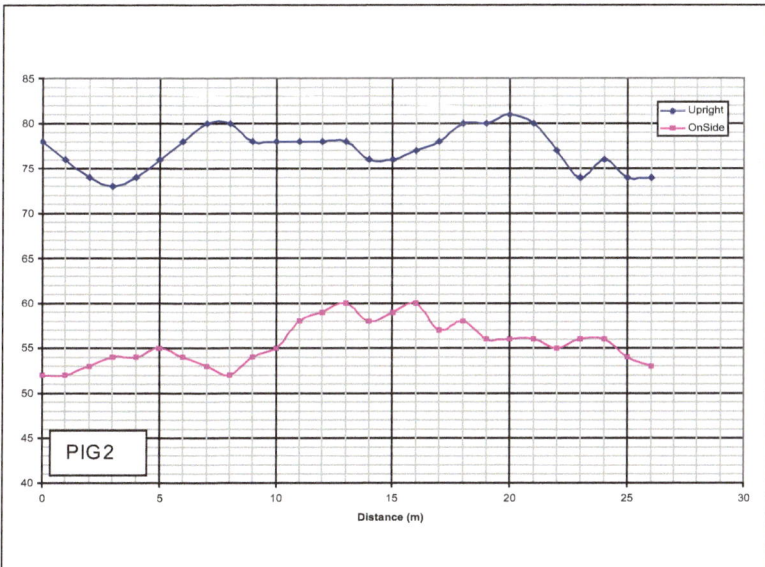

FIGURE 6.80
Pig site 2 EM results. Vertical and horizontal readings are shown.

The electromagnetic conductivity results for kangaroo site 1 showed an increase in conductivity coincident with the grave (at 15 m) for the horizontal readings (see Figure 6.79). The vertical readings showed a general decrease in overall conductivity over the area surveyed. The horizontal reading was more sensitive at shallower depths.

It was expected that within the grave area there would be an indication of higher conductivity (because of moisture retention within the grave area) compared with the surrounding soil. Dissolved ions create the potential for higher conductivity in the grave area. Correspondingly, a lower resistivity reading within a grave area would be expected.

Pig site 2 showed an increase in conductivity for the horizontal reading at the location of the grave (approximately 15 m) that then declined with distance away from the pig grave (Figure 6.80). The upright reading, however, showed a slight decrease in conductivity at the location of the grave.

The shallow buried pig was closer to the surface and the upcast would not retain moisture well under the hot and dry conditions. At this upper level, it is possible previous rains may have washed any dissolved ions away that could have affected conductivity levels.

The EM results showed increases in conductivity coincident with both the kangaroo and pig graves for the horizontal readings. This was more distinctive for the kangaroo site than the pig site and the overall readings were higher at the kangaroo site. The differences in survey results between the pig and kangaroo burial may be due to several factors:

- differences in length of burial, as the kangaroos had been buried for almost 2 years compared with the pigs, which had only been buried for a few months
- REDOX zonation away from the body
- difference in depth at which the bodies were buried (the kangaroo was buried at 1 m compared with the 0.4 m depth of the pig), and
- effect of burrowing on the survey readings. The pig site had been more extensively burrowed than the kangaroo site.

Electromagnetic Survey 2

An EM38, electromagnetic induction meter was used to assess the conductivity levels at each of the six animal gravesites, the first human grave and the calibration pit (in December 2003). The second human body had not been buried at this time.

The electromagnetic induction meter used for these results is shown in Figure 6.81 (EM38).

A grid system was drawn up over each grave using coloured marker points at which sites the EM readings were taken. Readings were taken from nine points over each animal grave (three across by three down), with the middle point of the grid being the centre of each grave. For the animal graves, an extra reading was taken resting flat on the middle of each animal grave, as well as the one level with the surface (holding it above the centre of the burrowed area). Random sample readings (at 12 positions) were also taken from within the animal grave area. The Global Positioning System (GPS) provided the positions of each reading at the animal sites.

Upright (vertical) and flat (horizontal) readings were taken at each point. In the vertical position, the most sensitive depth was 0.75 m compared with the shallower most sensitive depth of 0.3 m in the horizontal position. All measurements were taken in decisiemens.

The sample readings of the animal grave area at Roseworthy in both the horizontal and vertical positions showed variation across the field (see Table 6.10). The mean of the shallow or horizontal reading was 0.37, with a range of 0.24 to 0.46. The mean of the deep or vertical reading was 0.53, with a range of 0.37 to 0.67.

The conductivity readings at kangaroo site 1 (see Table 6.11) for both the horizontal and vertical readings were above the means of the sample soil readings and above the highest readings in the sample ranges. The centre of

FIGURE 6.81
Electromagnetic induction meter (EM38).

TABLE 6.10
Electromagnetic Survey Results of Animal Grave Area (Random Soil Samples at
Roseworthy)

Horizontal (Emv)	Vertical (Emv)
0.29	0.44
0.41	0.66
0.44	0.65
0.46	0.67
0.37	0.58
0.43	0.58
0.39	0.55
0.36	0.52
0.32	0.47
0.37	0.51
0.35	0.50
0.24	0.41
	0.37
Mean 0.37	Mean 0.53

the grave showed the highest readings at both the horizontal and vertical
positions. The highest readings were obtained both when the readings were
taken level with the unburrowed surface (holding the instrument above the
burrowed ground surface level with the unburrowed surface) and when the
instrument was level with the burrowed surface (within the hole).

Tables 6.12 and 6.13 show the survey results for the animal graves
according to the position on the grave from which the readings were taken
(using a grid method overlaying the grave). The reading obtained when the
EM38 was positioned within the burrow is indicated in the table by the
centre row. Rows 1 and 3 are the results for each end of the grave. The
centre column has the reading points that are taken from the line of where
the body lays most directly. The columns either side are the results for the
readings spaced approximately 0.3 m either side of the centre of the
gravesites.

The readings for kangaroo site 2 (Table 6.12) are also above the
random soil sample readings taken from the area. The highest conductivity results were obtained from the centre of the burrow (coincident with
the centre of the grave).

The conductivity readings for kangaroo site 3 were not as high as for
sites 1 and 2. The horizontal readings were similar to the random soil
readings. The vertical readings were high at the centre of the grave and, in

TABLE 6.11
Kangaroo Site 1: Horizontal and Vertical EM38 Survey Results

Row	Horizontal (Emv)			Vertical (Emv)		
1	0.47	0.49	0.49	0.67	0.64	0.74
2	0.49	**0.51**	0.48	0.68	**0.78**	0.72
Centre*		**0.58**			**0.84**	
3	0.47	0.47	0.51	0.72	0.68	0.73

Note: *Each centre figure is the reading obtained from the middle of each burrow, when the electromagnetic induction meter was positioned nearest the ground. The middle figure in each row 2 is the reading obtained when the electromagnetic induction meter was level with the surface, over the middle of the burrow.

particular, when taken from the middle of the burrow, although they were not significantly higher than the samples and did not show the degree of difference from the samples that was evident at sites 1 and 2.

Conductivity readings at pig site 1 (Table 6.13) were significantly lower for the horizontal and vertical readings than the random soil sample readings. However, the two readings taken from the centre of the grave were higher than the surrounding readings.

Pig site 2 showed similar results to pig site 1 in that there was no significant difference compared with the random sample readings.

Pig site 3 was situated at the base of a tree. The conductivity readings, although higher than the mean for the random samples, were all within the range of those obtained for the random soil samples.

TABLE 6.12
Kangaroo Site 2: Horizontal and Vertical EM38 Survey Results

Row	Horizontal (Emv)			Vertical (Emv)		
1	0.43	0.38	0.42	0.67	0.59	0.62
2	0.40	**0.45**	0.42	0.63	**0.66**	0.61
Centre		**0.50**			**0.79**	
3	0.39	0.43	0.42	0.64	0.62	0.64

TABLE 6.13
Pig Site 1: Horizontal and Vertical EM38 Survey Results

Row	Horizontal (Emv)			Vertical (Emv)		
1	0.24	0.21	0.23	0.37	0.33	0.34
2	0.23	0.21	0.22	0.34	0.34	0.34
Centre		0.26			0.43	
3	0.23	0.22	0.21	0.34	0.31	0.34

The animal grave conductivity results showed higher vertical readings in numerical terms compared with the horizontal readings. Electrical conductivity showed potential for grave detection based on the results obtained for the kangaroo graves 1 and 2. The pig graves could not be detected using the electrical conductivity method. The differences in conductivity levels between the kangaroo and pig graves could be related to length of burial; at the time of the survey, the kangaroos had been buried for 4 years and 9 months, and the pigs for 3 years and 5 months. Furthermore, as the kangaroo graves had been buried for longer, the soil may have been more compacted, having had more time to settle, leading to a higher level of salts more densely packed within a smaller area. This would give a higher conductivity reading. It is more likely that the results differ because of the more extensive burrowing at the pig sites that were shallower than the kangaroo sites.

Kangaroo site 3 could not be detected using this method. It is more difficult to explain the lack of conductivity at kangaroo site 3 in comparison with the other two kangaroo sites. This site did not stand out against the background conductivity level of the area. This kangaroo was buried at the shallowest depth (0.59 m) and was the smallest kangaroo, which makes it more comparable with the pig graves. It is possible that the less original body mass and shallower grave does not lend itself to detection by this method. As this grave was located at the base of the tree, there may have been some influence from this source in terms of leaching moisture and any deposited ions.

Human Grave Site 1 and Calibration Pit

At the human gravesite 1 and calibration pit, readings were taken along a grid of 0.5 m spacings in both the vertical and horizontal positions. Within the caged compound containing the first human gravesite (site 1), 0.5 m spaced points were drawn on a grid using spray painted dots of six across by eight down. The position of the grid in relation to the mesh of the cage is shown in Figure 6.82. The grid was 0.7 m from the cage on the left (looking from the calibration end toward open space), 0.9 m from the right side of the cage, 1.35 m from the top end (where feet were buried) and 1.2 m from the back end of the cage (shown diagrammatically in Figure 6.82). For the calibration pit, readings were taken along a grid of six points across by seven points down. Additional readings were taken from the general burial area for background sampling purposes.

The conductivity readings here did not involve the use of a GPS unit because of the likely interference from the wire cage compound. Table

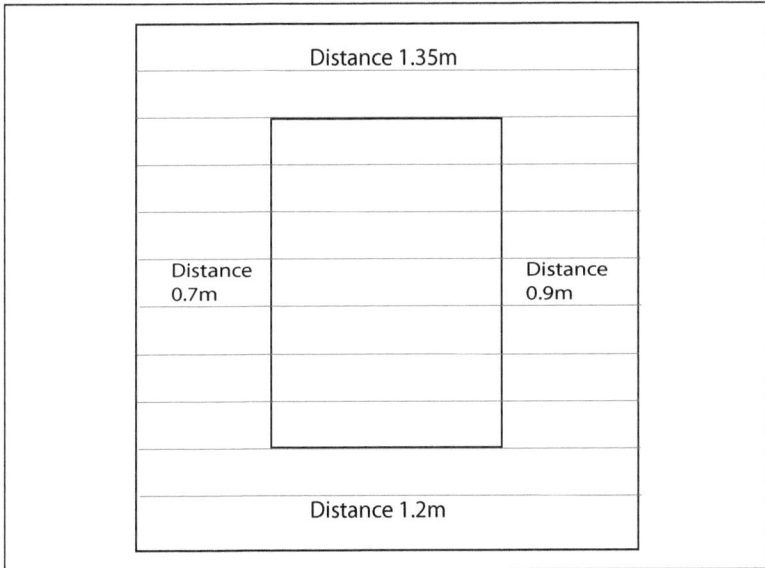

FIGURE 6.82
Electromagnetic induction meter (EM38).

6.14 shows the results of the random samples taken from the human burial site area (human burials and calibration pit).

Tables 6.15 and 6.16 record the results of the EM38 readings from the calibration pit and human gravesite 1, respectively. The graves are located in the two centre columns and each reading was taken at 0.5 m intervals. The shaded areas in the tables show the central points of the grave area.

TABLE 6.14
EM38 Results for Random Soil Samples at human burial area (December 2003)

Horizontal (Emv)	Vertical (Emv)
0.38	0.01
0.33	0.02
0.29	0.00
0.31	0.01
0.30	0.02
0.31	0.00
0.34	0.05
0.31	0.00
Mean 0.32	Mean 0.01

TABLE 6.15
EM38 Results for Calibration Pit

Horizontal readings (0.5 m spacings) (Emv)

0.38	0.40	0.40	0.41	0.42	0.41
0.34	0.35	0.35	0.36	0.35	0.34
0.33	0.31	**0.32**	**0.33**	0.32	0.18*
0.31	0.30	**0.31**	**0.30**	0.30	0.29
0.31	0.30	**0.30**	**0.29**	0.29	0.31
0.30	0.30	0.30	0.29	0.31	0.31
0.31	0.31	0.31	0.30	0.30	0.31

Vertical readings (0.5m spacings) (Emv)

0.07	0.07	0.08	0.08	0.10	0.09
0.04	0.30	0.04	0.02	0.04	0.05
0.01	0.02	**0.03**	**0.01**	0.01	0.02
0.01	0.03	**0.03**	**0.02**	0.00	0.01
0.00	0.01	**0.30**	**0.03**	0.01	0.00
0.01	0.00	0.00	–0.01	–0.01	0.00
0.00	0.00	0.00	0.00	0.00	0.00

Note: *A small anomaly was noted here and was considered most likely to be a rock.

TABLE 6.16
EM38 Results for Human Grave 1

Horizontal reading (0.5 m spacings) (Emv)

7.54	7.38	6.11	5.88	6.77	9.16
8.19	6.22	5.60	5.63	6.60	9.51
9.71	6.42	**5.63**	**5.39**	6.17	9.54
8.75	6.31	**4.94**	**4.85**	5.77	9.29
9.58*	5.53	**4.67**	**4.43**	5.40	8.84
7.75	5.88	**4.21**	**3.95**	4.75	7.92
6.82	5.90	4.22	3.99	4.51	7.63
6.36	5.71	4.52	4.21	4.76	7.03

Vertical reading (0.5m spacings) (Emv)

4.55	3.00	2.46	3.32	3.89	4.94
4.09	2.29	2.04	2.76	3.30	4.28
3.56	2.06	**2.06**	**3.16**	3.09	4.16
3.74	1.95	**2.83**	**3.86**	3.09	4.21
3.73	1.76	**2.62**	**3.85**	3.23	4.51
3.74	2.01	**2.38**	**3.92**	3.54	4.64
4.17	2.40	2.29	3.76	4.08	5.56
5.00	3.49	3.50	3.92	4.94	6.03

Note: *A metal pole supporting the cage was located beside this reading site.

The calibration pit showed little variation in the readings across the width of the pit, indicating little variation in conductivity between disturbed and undisturbed ground.

The conductivity readings taken at the human grave (Table 6.16) almost 2 years after burial were approximately five times higher for the horizontal readings than the calibration pit and approximately three times higher for the vertical readings. The bold numbers show the approximate area of the grave.

There was a significant difference between the values of the results of the calibration pit and the random samples compared with the human grave (site 1). The human grave in both the vertical and horizontal readings had a higher level of conductivity compared with both the random samples and the calibration pit. It is noted the conductivity values increased as the grid pointed near the position of the metal poles and wire cage.

The human gravesite 1 appeared to have been detected using electrical conductivity based on the significantly higher levels of conductivity coincident with the gravesite compared with both the calibration pit and the random sample readings. At this time, the human body had been buried for almost 2 years and the calibration pit was almost 1 year old. The conductivity values increased as the grid pointed near the position of the metal poles and wire cage, demonstrating an effect of the wire mesh on the conductivity readings. This means that it cannot be discounted that the result obtained for the human grave are related to the proximity of the metal. This method of ground surveying would need to be carried out again without the wire cage around the grave in order to arrive at any firm conclusions about the conductivity at human gravesite 1. As the calibration pit did not show any significant differences in conductivity from the surrounding area, any difference obtained at the human gravesite could be attributed to the characteristics of the grave itself and, in particular, its different contents.

7

Unearthing the Cultural Bases for Clandestine Graves

> *'So,' I said. 'Aren't there any rules the whole world can agree on?'*
> *The boy was triumphant. 'Killing people.'*

> Ian McEwan, *Enduring Love* (1997, p. 120)

In a world in which death is most often explained in medical terms, the clandestine grave, which is usually linked with a violent and unforeseen death, is an anathema. So far, this book has addressed clandestine graves from the more physical aspects. There are other less tangible aspects to consider; questions about why these graves are dug, what they might represent to the gravemaker and to the wider community, and what they tell us about societies in which this act was carried out. Do such considerations enable us to identify underlying factors that might be applied to body searches? Creating a clandestine grave is a deliberate act that derives from cultural or social learning, beliefs and expectations (as do all actions). This chapter extends the exploration of this social phenomenon that human beings persist in beyond its physical attributes. If, as Mary Douglas the anthropologist says, 'Everything we do is significant, nothing is without its conscious symbolic load. Moreover, nothing is lost on the audience' (Douglas, 1966, p. 121), then a clandestine grave will have or be vested with a significance to both the protagonist and the audience. We will see if we can describe this.

A clandestine grave is precipitated by an inadvertent or intended death. I refer to murder in its broadest terms here, because homicide includes murder and manslaughter (an accidental killing or killing in self-defence). Both can, in theory, be premeditated to some extent, and both can involve the disposal of a body. After killing someone, the perpetrator must choose whether to leave the body to be discovered or to hide it. If the body is to be hidden, the available options must first be perceived within any given environment. Environments have two aspects — the cultural (the social context) and the physical (the landscape). Our consideration of the cultural significance of the clandestine grave will be based on these two landscape systems.

Let us first trace the span of a clandestine grave's existence. Wherever, and however, the body is hidden, if discovery occurs (and this is not certain), it will either be by accident or through an investigation. If located, the event will most likely be disclosed to the public through the media. The body from the clandestine grave will then be transferred to what is deemed a more suitable place of deposit, either in a cemetery or cremated. The empty clandestine grave will be filled in and left. Once found, it is never marked as a primary burial place. This is the bare outline of our subject matter.

It is a curious observation that there is a great volume of written material on death, dying, funeral customs, cemeteries and changing perceptions of death over time that stand in contrast to a relative literary silence on the death practices linked to murder (although suicide is a subject of significant analysis). A large portion of studies dealing with death concentrate on exequies, or funereal practices, and concepts of death in modern society. Clandestine graves of the 'ordinary murder victim' do not generate the degree of interest that is seen in the search for the buried bodies of Tsar Nicholas II's children (such as the Princess Anastasia) or Che Guevara. The location of and reburial of victims of murder who do not have a celebrity status or public persona are not the subjects of politicisation such as that surrounding the bodies of Tsar Nicholas II's family. In 1991, the bodies were moved from a secret grave in Yekaterinberg, finally to be reburied in the St Petersburg family chapel in 1998 (Verdery, 1999). Nor is there the interest that is shown towards the mass graves such as those in North Korea, Chechnya or Fromelles.

The victim's corpse is an almost nonexistent subject in anthropological discourse, except where the corpse itself is a visible and public feature in its own right — for example, two notable studies by Verdery (1999) who discusses the meaning attributed to famous dead bodies, and Crossland (2009), who discusses the objectification of dead bodies in scientific practice, especially forensic anthropology, using as a starting point the way in which the remains of Ned Kelly, an Australian outlaw and hero figure have been used to interpret the dead, and 'produce the dead body'. These two studies are about historical figures, long dead, whose corpses have been given a public persona post-mortem.

Death as a result of murder is a subject that is most often discussed in terms of the sociopathology of the murderer. There are analyses of information that suggest patterns of behaviour to lead to an understanding of 'typified criminal behaviour'. For example, geographic or spatial analysis is a tool that has been applied retrospectively to homicide cases, most particularly to serial murders to link offender residence to body disposal sites. In the end, individual offender behaviour is difficult to predict and causal factors remain relatively speculative.

Interestingly, the single clandestine grave, if it is not part of a serial murder, is not the subject of data collections that might be used for research. This may be indicative of a tendency to view murder as an aberrant act stemming from individual 'malfunction'. We have not acknowledged that murder continues to be inflicted on others, and that bodies are actively hidden by different individuals, sometimes in inventive ways that require considerable effort. How this is related to cultural factors has not been explored. Are there cultural factors that inhibit this behaviour in some societies or suggest it in others as a solution to a situation, either directly or inadvertently?

For now, let's return to considering what goes into creating a clandestine grave. There is a pragmatic side to disposing of a body. A murderer is generally directly responsible for the disposal and handling of the body, and to minimise the risk of exposure, avoids input from too many others. We must remember that most people in contemporary industrialised societies have no direct contact with dead bodies unless they are in a medical, scientific, emergency service, coronial or funereal related professions. The murderer will either have no support systems for this situation, or will rely on others with a similar desire to avoid judicial consequences, or who may be coerced into participating in an act that has potential judicial consequences. The cultural landscape for the disposer of a body is a limited sphere of interaction.

To dispose of the body via a clandestine grave, the murderer will have needed to choose a site for the unmarked grave. We can assume the choice of burial site will be moderated by both perceptions about those landscapes and pragmatic opportunity. There are a number of speculative factors that could relate to the selection of burial or disposal site; distance from the death site, delay after death before burial, preparedness to travel to dispose of the body and what constitutes an area that is unlikely for the body to be discovered. Further, there could be a symbolic element to the gravemaker of what constitutes a suitable disposal site.

What are the physical settings for clandestine graves? Clandestine graves have been found in a variety of environmental settings, both urban (in backyards, vacant blocks) and more nonresidential areas (national parks, unused tracts of land, scrubland). For obvious practical reasons, the murderer is unlikely to travel interstate or overseas with the body. Therefore, sites for such graves tend to be selected within the confines of an environment that is within travelling distance and allows transport of the body. We will return to where bodies have been hidden later in this chapter.

Considering the practical elements, disposal of a body should ideally take into account factors such as the commencement of decay, the subsequent odours emitted and the possible attraction of scavenging animals. The body could be moved from one storage place or burial to another, but this requires effort and increases both the potential of being observed and also leaving additional evidence linking the murderer to the crime. Moving a body, of course, also requires identifying further places or means of disposal. The range of body disposal methods may be broadly categorised as follows, and each has associated risks or disadvantages:

- Storage: the risk of discovery must be minimised. Murder victims in Australian cases have been found stored in freezers, large barrels and cemented in wheelie bins used for rubbish. Storage of the body may also involve dismemberment in order to store body parts separately or in smaller areas.

- Cremation: burning human remains requires consideration of fire restrictions in Australia (and avoiding drawing attention to the act) or having access to a suitable furnace, and it would be unlikely for the bones to be completely destroyed in this way. Ashes of course, would be easier to dispose of.

- Hidden in the environment: bodies have been placed in 'out of the way' areas, not readily seen by people, such as beneath logs, under leaves or bushes, in dams, rivers, oceans, lakes in national parks, reserves, or scrubland, in dumps and landfill sites. Burial in a clandestine grave falls within this category.

- Direct attempts at destruction and reduction through such means as the application of chemicals or use of tools or machinery.

How does a clandestine grave compare with other options for body disposal within the contemporary urban landscape?

- A clandestine grave is less likely to be discovered in areas where people do not frequent.

- Availability of bush, scrubland or areas such as national parks that are not owned and tended as private concerns provide sites in which a body might be hidden and unnoticed or digging goes unremarked.

- Scavengers (such as dingoes, crocodiles and foxes) may dispose of bodies in more remote areas (although bones may be exposed).

- Burial in an area not directly associated with the victim or murderer will lessen the likelihood of a causal association and discovery of the body.

- Hiding the body delays discovery and no one knows murder has occurred for sure. It also allows time for the murderer to invent a story or vacate the investigation zone.

- Burial does not require sophisticated equipment, and the instruments used are likely to be available or easily accessed or purchased (shovel, pick and a car for transport) and later disposed of without undue notice.

It may be that burial in a clandestine grave is perceived as a simpler task than other forms of disposal. In reality, burying a body is a cumbersome and energy taxing task. It involves finding an unobtrusive place of burial, transporting the body (or live victim) to the place of burial, obtaining digging implements, excavating the grave (which is physically demanding and time consuming), carrying the body to the hole and avoiding witnesses during the entire process.

Interestingly, for such a serious act with serious consequences, police consider that in most cases of burial there is very little preparation beforehand for the disposal of the body (from personal communications with police). The Federal Bureau of Investigation in the United States analysed the common characteristics of clandestine graves based on collected information over a 10-year period (1993–2003). The common traits were:

- the depth of the burials was under a 1 m (between 0.5 and 0.76 m)

- sites selected for burials were typically a short distance from infrequently travelled roads or pathways

- clandestine graves were generally located approximately 3 m from the closest large tree and were usually surrounded by bushes or heavy foliage

- the body was usually clothed or wrapped in plastic and was positioned face down within the grave

- the average age of the clandestine graves at the time of the search was between 4 and 6 years (Dulgerian, N., '2003 Internal Report of the FBI Laboratory, Evidence Response Team Unit, Evaluation of Technology-Assisted Search Team Activities During 1993–2003' cited in Hoffman et al., 2009).

This kind of information is needed across contemporary industrialised countries, and should be extended to consider other features, such as how far the perpetrator travelled or distance from the death site.

How Many Bodies Might be Buried in Clandestine Graves?

There have been many cases in Australia (and indeed most countries) of murdered persons whose bodies have been found in shallow graves and isolated places, such as fields, national parks or scrubland. It is a method of disposal that has been used by perpetrators when they have caused one death or more than one, for example, the infamous Truro murders in South Australia and the Claremont serial killings in Western Australia.

We would like to know how often this method of body disposal is used after the act of murder. Statistics on where bodies have been disposed of or how they were located are not centrally or systematically collated in Australia. Establishing the frequency of the burial of murder victims is not an easy task, but we will consider two sources of information that may provide some parameters of the magnitude of such incidences in Australia.

To give a context, approximately 35,000 people are reported missing each year in Australia or 1.5 persons per 1000 Australians out of a total population of approximately 21.5 million, of which 99% are found (Dearden and Jones, 2008). This leaves around 300 people who are not found each year, of which a proportion of these can be assumed to have been victims of murder. In 2006–2007, there were 260 homicide victims in Australia and 296 homicide offenders (Davies and Mouzos, 2007). Most of the victims were male (185 compared with 81 female) and most of the offenders were male (242 compared with 54 female). The rate of intimate-partner homicide was calculated as being 22%. Twenty-seven children under the age of 15 years were killed in 2006–2007, most by a parent (84%). Of these victims, it is unknown what proportion were buried, presumably because it is not of sufficient interest. Similar figures have been reported for California, with 37,918 adults reported missing in 2007. Of these, 459 were missing under suspicious circumstances. Over 350 missing persons in California were found deceased in each year of 2006, 2007 and 2008 (White, 2009).

Where is the raw information about clandestine burials or body disposals to be sourced? To properly quantify details about buried bodies and how they are located would require going through individual police files held by the branches all over Australia, which would obviously be a daunting task. The logistics of raw data collection on clandestine grave cases was highlighted in Chapter 5.

Australian newspaper articles featuring human bodies and/or skeletal remains being found in Australia during the calendar years 2000–2004 proved a useful source of complementary information. Murders are always considered newsworthy; they convey messages of possible public danger, inform the public of the death of a person, generate interest in events that are generally outside most people's experience and prompt those who may have information about the death to come forward. The figures from the tabloid incidences do not provide a total count of all bodies disposed of in clandestine graves in the selected period for several reasons; first, the figures cannot include those not found and second, there may be cases that are purposefully not made known to the media by police for investigative reasons. Murders may have occurred during the selected time period, with the bodies remaining unlocated, in which case there would be no report of a body found in the media.

The relevant tabloid reports were sourced from the internet using the Factiva search engine and excluding various cases (such as repeat articles, those bodies found immediately after being murdered with no attempt made to hide the body and usually left at the site of the murder, remains washed up on beaches or found in rivers, suicide cases and occasions of accidental death). From this search, there were 184 reported findings of human remains that were not immediately located after death or their known disappearance over this 4-year period across Australia (Table 7.1). Some of the bodies reported in the tabloids were those of victims that had been murdered before 2000. Particular factors noted were the environment type in which bodies were found (such as backyards and national parks), how they had been found, and how long after the murder had occurred that the bodies had been found.

Of the 184 bodies found between 2000 and 2004 as reported by the media, the majority, 170 bodies, had been found within 12 months from the time of death. Two bodies were located 2 years after being murdered; one after 3 years; two after 4 years; one after 5 years, two after 7 years and one body was found 78 years after death (or being reported missing). These figures from public tabloid articles only cite cases of located bodies and not the total the number of murders that occurred during this period. This data is summarised in Table 7.1.

Where Are the Clandestine Graves Found?

Most of the bodies (154 or 84%) found in this period were located in outer metropolitan or remote areas (Table 7.1). There were 98 bodies located in what was described in the articles as bushland, national parks or reserves. Thirteen bodies were described specifically as having been

TABLE 7.1
Locations of Missing Bodies Found 2000–2004 as Reported in All Australian Tabloids (Australian Tabloid Reports of Bodies)

Location type	Number of bodies found*	Description
Outer metropolitan or remote areas		
Bushland	69	6 of these were in bushland in the suburbs
Reserves/state forest	21	
Shallow graves	8	6 in bushland, 1 in recreation area, 1 on beach
Deep graves	1	In reserve
Mangroves/wetlands	3	1 wetlands
Country road	12	Found by or in close proximity to a road
River, lagoon	10	Found in a river/lagoon itself
River bank	3	
Creek	9	Found in a creek bed (often dry)
Swamp	1	
Quarry	3	
Dam	3	Found in remote property dams
Cliff base	3	
Underwater cave	1	
In car on property	6	Bodies within cars in remote areas
Drain	1	
Metropolitan areas		
Shallow graves	4	4 in backyards
Suburban (street, backyard near river, buildings)	13	4 in parklands,
Golfcourse	2	
Mangroves	2	
Garbage tip	4	
In wheelie bin	3	1 was cemented into the bin
Drain	2	
Total	**184**	

Note: *All figures cited are separate individuals and are not double counted in other location categories.

buried. This does not mean just 13 victims were buried, but rather that the article did not specify the circumstances of many other bodies discovered. Eight of these specifically reported burials were in shallow graves in remote or scrub areas (one was on a beach). One was in a deep grave (approximately 1.5–2.0 m) and four burials were in suburban backyards.

How were the bodies found? The newspaper articles did not provide many details about the circumstances of the locations, and most often it simply read that a body had been 'found'. Table 7.2 shows that just over half (56%) of the articles did not state how the bodies had been found. A significant proportion (35%) of the bodies found were accidentally located by passers-by or people in the course of their work (such as farmers, roadworkers or park rangers). This percentage could be higher if they include a portion of those 'not stated' in the articles. Police were reported to have located only 8% (two accidentally and four of these cases through an informant). There were two bodies found by Aboriginal trackers while they were searching for another victim (not those bodies found). There was one description of the use of ground penetrating radar to search the cemented base of a pool under which it was suspected a body was buried, but this was unsuccessful.

It is important not to overcritique the source of data. The detail about how the bodies had been found may not have been seen as significant or known to the journalist, and police sometimes limit the disclosure of detail about a case as part of their investigative strategies.

From this highly public source of information, the principal methods that lead to the discovery of a buried body are accidental discovery (passers-by or bushwalkers, other accidental discoveries by people in the course of their work) and informants providing knowledge to the police. Proactive search methods do not feature in these reports as a principal means for locating murder victims. This does not mean different search methods are not used during police searches, but rather that the tabloid reports only mentioned 'discoveries'. The majority (103 cases of discoveries) did not state how the bodies were found. Discovery of the body was the object of the report.

The majority of the bodies (98) found in these reports, were located in what was described as bushland, national parks or reserves, away from metropolitan areas. It is of interest that there were 12 bodies found relatively close to country roads, suggesting some attempt to dispose of the bodies away from the metropolitan zone, but they were not well-hidden. There is an irony that although being deposited in scrubland or bush areas with what would be expected to have minimal pedestrian traffic, the majority of bodies were discovered by accident by passers-by or bushwalkers. Does this mean disposers of bodies are not familiar with walking trails and bushwalkers' habits?

It is feasible that hiding the body is only part of the object of the disposer and that part of the disposal purpose may be to add an element of randomness to the discovery to distance the perpetrator from the crime.

TABLE 7.2
Means of Finding Bodies 2000–2004 (as Reported in Australian Tabloids)

Means of location	Number of bodies	Comments
Passers-by/bushwalkers	49	
Workers	15	In the course of people's work activity
Police	14	4 found through a 'tip-off', 2 found while on a different case
Aboriginal trackers	2	
Clairvoyant	1	Family of a missing person engaged a clairvoyant
Not stated	103	
Total	184	

Other cases of burial may well be more deliberate in the intent to bury and hide, so the bodies are not discovered by accident. These data compare with recent unpublished research in Florida. A survey was sent to Florida police jurisdictions about the recovery of human remains between 1990 and 2000. Out of 366 agencies, just 38 responded, reporting a total of 73 recoveries. Of these, 39 were found by accident. Of those buried, most were shallow burials (4 ft and shallower), and most bodies were found in what was classified as remote or wooded areas (Hays, 2008). There are aspects of the place of deposit that need further consideration, such as the proximity of place of deposit to the place of murder. Clearly, many of the bodies in the preceding tabloid data were those that were discovered. There may well be another type of category not so readily discovered.

The physical landscape is used by the body disposer to conceal the body, but it also dislocates the body in place and time to an accessible anonymous area. Culturally influenced behaviours are carried out within the physical landscape (Hardesty, 1941), and scrubland is a common environment for the clandestine grave. In Australia, it is easy to reach scrubland from any city, including scrubland in national parks and reserves. Scrubland, bush or reserve areas may be more representative of areas with no ready association to the perpetrator, and of course are accessible (and easier to drive to in periods with no visitors). In these respects, the national park or reserve area could have an attraction as a place for depositing a body. Broad tracts of public land (national parks) are found in many parts of the modern industrialised world, and they vary according to climate and landscape use. For example, Australian national parks tend to be much wilder (overgrown and less tended) than some other countries, such as those in the United Kingdom.

In terms of concealment, there are other examples of possibly more effective methods of disposal that were found in the tabloid articles, such as the use of wheelie bins that are now emptied by robotic trucks (minimising immediate discovery); dams on remote properties, quarries, and in abandoned cars on properties.

What can we begin to make of this information? Clandestine graves are one of a variety of methods to dispose of a body. Such methods reflect environmental opportunities (the physical landscape) and use of these opportunities may be a function of past experience, collaboration or perceived haste or time available (cultural landscape), or planning. There are common features to the places in which bodies are found buried. These are secluded, off (not necessarily far away) well-trodden paths and within driving access. Bodies tend not to be buried in open areas with no foliage, or where there is the likelihood of development or excavation work.

Case Files of Body Disposal

Below are briefly described some examples of bodies placed in a clandestine grave or concealed. Examples of the use of clandestine graves are easy to find in newspaper reports. From these cases can be seen the variety of disposals, both in terms of victims, method and selection of disposal site.

The Claremont serial murders in Western Australia occurred in 1996 and 1997. Three women disappeared from a wealthy suburb, and two bodies were later found in bushland areas in, outer suburbs of Perth. One body was not found.

In 2002, the bodies of a wealthy couple, Margaret Wales-King and Paul King, were found in a single shallow grave in the Yarra Ranges National Park outside of Melbourne. The grave was in a clearing between trees. They were found by a walker, who thought it was a bird's nest.

A young boy, Graeme Thorne, was kidnapped in 1960. The murderer drove the body to a vacant block and placed the body under an overhanging ledge amidst low scrub, but only 20 m from the road. Two months later, the body was found by children.

In 2001 in South Australia, the body of a young girl was found by a police search in a large, industrial rubbish dump. The remains were found in no small part because of the detailed records of when waste was deposited and the sectioning of dumps.

In 2008 in Australia, a young child (aged 3 years) was murdered by his father while on a road trip. There were extreme difficulties in identifying the place where the body might have been deposited. The search involved aerial surveillance and the body was located through narrowing the area by surveillance television (sites such as service stations in which the child was sighted in the vehicle) and landmark information from the perpetrator. This narrowed the zone to one in which there were still many mineshafts. The body was found within a deep mineshaft (approximately 7 m deep) through the use of lowered mirrors.

Dismembering increases the difficulties of body location and resolving the murder. In 2001, parts of a murder victim were found buried in a vegetable garden near the victim's home (torso parts), the head in a drum in an urban industrial area, the main torso in outer metropolitan scrubland and the limbs in a national park in an outer metropolitan zone of Adelaide. The body parts were located primarily through information provided by the murderer.

In a further case of dismembering (2009), a woman perpetrator deposited parts of an elderly victim near the murderer's home in common walking scrubland, placed under bushes and wrapped in plastic. Not all parts of the victim's body have been located at this time.

Figures 7.1 and 7.2 show a crime scene in which a body was located in a forest area in South Australia. The body was covered with pine branches and had been scavenged by animals.

FIGURE 7.1
Site of body location in a forest area in South Australia.
Source: SA Police, published with permission.

FIGURE 7.2
Remains found in a forest area in South Australia.
Source: SA Police, published with permission.

These are all examples of murders followed by body disposals. They highlight the widely varying places of clandestine graves and body disposal, precipitated by a pragmatism and environmental opportunism. This pragmatism is a response to the cultural landscape in which this is carried out.

The Law and Clandestine Graves

In contemporary industrialised societies like Australia, the act of killing someone is illegal and constitutes a crime; an act not sanctioned by society that incurs consequences intended as deterrents. In such societies, murder is defined as the most severe crime in terms of the degree of punishment able to be passed to the perpetrator. Laws regarding murder are supposed to inhibit people from acting on instincts and emotional urges to permanently destroy a person, and to provide some safeguard that we, in the society, will not be killed at the whim of another because of the consequences that follow the transgression of this law. Yet, this law like many other laws is obviously transgressed by members of society on a continuing basis. Clandestine graves, acts of hiding of a body, are indicative of a consciousness of the overriding social order.

Murder is obviously a crime, but once committed, what are the laws (explicit rules) associated with how the victim's body is treated? Offences against the dead are termed thanatological crimes. When people die, the deaths are to be registered under the Births, Deaths and Marriages Registration Act 1996 in South Australia. There are laws about where and how the deceased may be disposed, and the treatment of the body. The *Transplantation and Anatomy Act 1983* prohibits the removal of tissue from the body of a deceased person without appropriate authorisations in South Australia.

It is generally held that dead bodies have the right to a suitable burial and the right (through the survivor) to select the place of burial. It is illegal to cremate a body in South Australia other than in a licensed crematorium (Crematorium Act 1891). The burial of bodies in areas other than cemeteries in Australia (and many industrial countries) contravenes legislation at the state and federal levels. Cemeteries themselves are largely governed by Local Government legislation in Australia, while health regulations apply to the burial of bodies in areas other than cemeteries. A notable exception is the burial of Kerry Packer, who was Australia's richest man, because he was buried in 2006 on his family property in the Hunter Valley.

Specifically to our interest, the *Criminal Code Act Compilation Act 1913* (section 215) refers to the interfering with a corpse to hinder enquiry. This section of the Act defines interfering with a corpse as concealing the corpse by burying it or destroying it (or 'otherwise'), or damaging or mutilating the corpse. It also includes reference to interfering with the corpse to circumvent investigations surrounding the death of the victim. An example of the upholding of such laws is found in a news article in June 2009 about a case in the United Kingdom in which a woman was alleged to have kept the remains of three infants hidden in a box in her house for up to 8 years. The woman was charged with three counts of indignity to a body and three counts of disposing of a child's body.

Does the body have rights or do persons associated with the body have rights over its treatment? Early English law held that dead bodies were not 'property' as they did not have intrinsic value and were not articles of commerce (derived from Sir Edward Coke). The corpse was not regarded as a subject of larceny (Johnson, 2000). In Australia, there has been some qualification to this law; in case law there is authority for the proposition that a dead body may become the subject of property where 'human skill' has been applied that is seen as differentiating it from a 'mere corpse awaiting burial' (Johnson, 2000, p. 27). The 'no property' rule aimed to protect the entitlement for a corpse to be interred appropriately through an absence of property rights. In the 'quasi-property rule', the next of kin may have some empowerment to affect the decent interment of relatives (Johnson, 2000). This quasi-property rule has been used in Australia and the United States.

Graves that contain the bodies of murder victims can remain undiscovered for weeks, months or years. When discovered, the significance of the human remains lies in first, proving above all that a murder has been committed or that a death has been concealed, and second, providing information about the fate of the missing person. The body becomes important as evidence and can link the murderer with the crime. The act of murder cannot be fully understood or proved without the body or some critical part of a body. Hence, the term corpus delicti or 'body of the crime'. In rare instances, convictions have occurred without a body but this is more difficult.

The Cultural Basis for Clandestine Graves

Burying a body is not a random occurrence. There is no doubt that the creation of a clandestine grave is an act outside of contemporary norms, as it is intrinsically linked to murder. Yet the rationality associated with this behaviour is disconcerting. How is this unacceptable piece of behaviour produced in the form that it assumes? How it is that digging a clandestine grave after killing a person is culturally transmitted? Tracing the roots of the act of digging a clandestine grave for a murder victim is a complex task, because it is not a subject that lends itself to ethnography, a strong basis for anthropological study. Indeed, one of the aspects that remains to be established is whether hiding a body is intended before the death.

Cultural learning (internalised knowledge) has its origins in the individual's exposure to family practices and the practices with which individuals are associated through communities. In many situations, the principle of uniformitarianism will govern behaviour, which states that when confronted with similar situations, people behave in fundamentally similar ways (Hole & Heizer, 1965). This would seem too simplistic an explanation for murder. Murder is difficult to consider as a situation or experience that individuals respond to from experience. It is more likely to be drawn from sources that are culturally embedded. From this perspective, when it comes to disposing of a body, a murderer will determine the options based on related (extrapolated) experience, knowledge (including cultural learning), inference, opportunity, environment and a varying element of deliberate consideration or planning.

Extensive diversity exists in contemporary societies, and smaller groups have shared sets of rules that govern behaviour (Gibbons, 1984). Some subgroups choose to regularly transgress certain laws. There are those sections of society that may be desensitised to murder (notably those familiar with the availability and access to hit men, to undertake paid murders to 'address a situation'). This more immediate setting is likely to be an important source of explanatory information, but is beyond the scope of this present study.

Are there contemporary parallel examples of sanctioned behaviour that might relate to the act of creating a grave? Perhaps the question is better phrased as how do we dispose of remains that confront us directly? Four examples came to mind. First, the burial of family pets in little used corners of backyards or other places intended not to be regularly traversed, such as fields or scrubland. If a pet could not be flushed down the toilet, it was buried in the suburban backyard. The remains were not suitable for the family trash because of the smell and attraction of ants, flies or dogs. A discreet hole in the ground was dug at the back of the property, indicating that burial is an acceptable informal method of disposal of the remains. Such burials are also not considered easements on properties when sold, nor generally disclosed. Second, the bones of babies have been found beneath housing floorboards or in gardens during renovations or demolitions. These may have been stillbirths, babies that died unexpectedly, possibly unwanted and murdered, but clearly not formally buried in ritual fashion, for reasons linked to expense, shame or hiding an unwanted child. Stillborn children were not required to be registered in South Australia until 1937, and there was no requirement for them to be buried in a cemetery (Nicol, 1994). Many were simply buried in the garden. Third, from the early days of Australia's settlement, there have been burials of people on family properties. Fourth, there is the customary burial in a cemetery, which is the more widely understood way of disposing of a body. These are all examples of cultural practices used to dispose of dead remains that are more or less familiar to those within a contemporary Australian society. These deaths would not all be the subjects of searches for the remains.

There are neutral and public sources of information that offer vicarious experience to murderers in the disposal of a body. Murder has become a common subject and there are readily accessible sources of information about the disposal of a body, such as books, novels, television, internet articles, newspapers and graphic novels. True crime sections in bookshops testify to its popularity. By way of example as to how such information can provide a source of 'learning', an article based on an interview with a person who murdered his mother and her husband in Australia states that the murderer based his plan of murdering the couple by drugging them from a 'cheap movie' (Crooks, 2005). He later hired a trailer, wrapping the bodies in a quilt, and drove the bodies to a national park and buried them in a shallow grave. Regardless of whether the movie provided method, the statement points to a common, accessible pool of knowledge within the cultural landscape.

Killing a person is an act that we are accustomed to viewing as unthinkable under any circumstances. Yet, we also know it happens and with varying degrees of deliberation. Sometimes none. This is not the place for a discussion of the motivations or reasons for murder, except to highlight that we risk assuming or at least overemphasising the causes or prompts. For the murderer, the killing of a person may be an action rather than a crime, as explained by the novelist Julian Burnside in his novel *The Devil's Footprint* (2007):

> An odd idea for anybody to have, that he is about to do something criminal. A man goes out to rob a bank, or kill somebody, or cash a stolen cheque, and he is doing exactly that thing, he doesn't think he is going out to commit a crime. The crime part of it is by the by. (p. 150)

It is the link between the circumstances of murder and the burial of bodies in clandestine graves, or more broadly, the act of hiding a body, that is little understood. The personage or representativeness of the victim to the perpetrator may or may not be significant in the decision to bury the body in a clandestine grave. For example, is the body more likely to be hidden when the victim is unknown to the killer, or if the victim was killed out of anger, or if the victim is in some way representative to the killer? Or is burial only linked to a need to conceal the death? Placing the body in an unmarked grave could be a symbolic burial of the murder act and a distancing of self from the victim.

Whoever the victim was or represented to the killer, in the case of a clandestine grave, the remaining body is an object to be discarded or hidden. Burying a body could be argued to function as a way of disconnecting the body from the perpetrator and from the implications of the act. Without the body that provides its own attestation as to cause of death, it is difficult to prove death rather than disappearance and disappearance followed by misadventure. Burying the body allows the murderer to continue to 'belong'. No one in authority knows of the act.

The burial of bodies after death is a longstanding practice. The burial of evidence of a crime also has a longstanding history. How does one begin to unravel the cultural precursors within a diverse cultural milieu such as Australia, a colonised and multicultural society?

The Place of Burial

Primarily, a clandestine grave is the burial of a body alone in a noncemetery setting. It is evocative of the bush burial, a familiar term in Australia. The body in the bush is identified as a cultural theme in artwork and tradition. Fitzpatrick has identified three dynamics in artworks about death in Australia; land, solitary death and the discovery of the corpse in the bush (1997, p. 22). Jalland (2002) describes the bush burial as a particularly Australian tradition, originating with the early European colonists, that had its own ritual separate from British traditions. Jalland posits 'the grave in the Australian bush became an important cultural image in its own right, establishing a sense of national identity and individual belonging …' (2002, p. 8), adding that the bush was the most distinctive and formative of Australian environments.

Many rural settlers were buried in typically shallow graves, not marked by stones (Awofeso, 2003). Those going into unchartered land were buried by co-travellers in unmarked or poorly marked graves. Sometimes their bodies were never found. The bush deaths, lonely graves and corpses buried were often not accompanied by much ritual (Jalland, 2002), compared with that in the 'home country'.

Bushland, a place from which many did not return, incorporated the idea of wildness, natural mystery and was 'the land of the never-never'. The image of lost children in the bush was powerful; 'The great nightmare of the colonial imagination in 19th century Australia was the vision of the innocent Anglo-Australian child lost in the alien vastness of the Australian bush' (Jalland, 2002, p. 287). Further, a concurrent part of Australia's historical cultural images of death were those that were described as masculine and frequently violent. Jalland cites examples in the bushman, the bushranger and the Anzac war fighter.

This imagery offers parallels between an isolated bush burial, or 'lonely grave', and the body buried in a clandestine (unmarked) grave. It suggests a cultural precedent or receptiveness to this type of practice. Australia, of course, is not the only place in which bodies are buried in scrubland or wilderness areas, but this way of disposing of a body hearkens back to the less ordered practices associated with burial without the professions with which we are familiar today. The clandestine grave can only represent an unexpected and crude death, and hurried anonymous burial that is actually congruent with earlier burial practices.

How do we deal with our 'dead human capital', to borrow a phrase used by Verdery (1999)? The establishment of cemeteries and church burial grounds in the newly colonised country reflects a surprisingly unsystematic way of burying bodies. In Adelaide, relatives had to dig the graves of loved ones (Nicol, 1988). During the 19th century, the early years of the South Australian colony, the dead were initially buried in 'any convenient spot' and this included singular isolated burials (Nicol, 1994). The cemeteries loosely designated as such in regional townships were described as wilderness areas with no provision for positioning graves and graves were most often shallow, being no deeper than a metre. Graves of individuals could not always be located properly after burial. Views on the disposal of human remains changed in most European societies from the 1830s, in particular, as attention was given to the management of cemeteries (Nicol, 1988), largely prompted by complaints about shallow and haphazardly placed burials, sometimes unmarked, and instances of animals scavenging graves.

There is no cult of the dead in contemporary industrialised society. Dead bodies are, in the end, objects to be disposed of in one way or another. There is an ambiguity around the fact that the disposal of human remains must be undertaken in ways that are also used for refuse collection (such as burial or burning, and allowed to biodegrade), yet we do not equate dead bodies with refuse (Awofeso, 2003). A body has no place in the social order and must be disposed of as something that is 'unclean' (however revered in life and now missed) in anthropologist Mary Douglas' terms (1966). The growing trend to develop ecofriendly cemeteries is an identifiable irony in comparison to the clandestine grave. For example, the options range from proposals to bury bodies vertically, to burial without a coffin to promote decomposition, and to situate these cemeteries in natural settings that are not as manicured as cemeteries have been in the recent past.

Death practices can be symbolic and ritualised, and change over time. Burial rituals have many particular purposes for different peoples, such as creating a capacity for the transcendence of the soul of the dead, maximising the chances of the person's resurrection, or minimising the risk of retribution from the deceased's spirit. For some Aboriginal Australian people, burial rituals prevent haunting by the ghost of the dead person. For Aboriginal Australian people today, cemeteries, although not always a feature of Aboriginal life, provide a family tree, a place of ancestors, in which spatial relationships of graves is important. Where a body is buried in a clandestine grave, these post-mortem aspects are not accorded to the victim. The choice for death-related rituals is the prerogative of the deceased through a legal will or the next of kin, and not the perpetrator of a clandestine grave.

To contrast burial in a clandestine grave with key aspects of what might be termed a socialised death ritual, we can identify several key differences:

- Presentation of the dead is an important part of the funerary ritual. The body placed in a clandestine grave is not washed or prepared, but is buried as they were killed. Usually on death, the corpse is tended by professionals, who aim to present the body before burial in as lifelike in appearance, in repose.

- In the 'usual' burial or funereal processes, there is a degree of personalisation that directly recognises the identity of the corpse as they were in life, beginning with the use of the memorial plaque or headstone (whether cremation or burial). In the United States, most forms of burial display an increasing emphasis on personalisation that is considered to reflect a growth in individualism (Collier, 2003). One could argue that this reflects a growing segmentation of society, in which individuals have fewer strong links, which creates a need to reinforce who an individual was in the face of a risk of anonymity. Patently, the clandestine grave is a burial that has no memorial, because there is an intended anonymity.

- Grave space was not purchased for the dead body by the murderer and until found, the corpse is not able to be processed through the usual rituals by those that take ownership of the body and are called on to make decisions about the body.

- No gravegoods are placed in the grave for sentimental reasons. We have difficulty with the clandestine grave, because there is no 'group rite'. It occurs with no more participation than that of the murderer.

- A clandestine grave also means it is difficult to refer to the dead as having 'passed away', 'passed over' or 'departed', because the death was clearly violent.

- A further contrast is that the victim's remains are not 'housed' collectively with the 'dead citizenry' or others from their society in a clandestine grave.

- The location of the clandestine grave has no significant attachment to place for the victim or the victim's social affiliations; the place of burial was the killer's choice. In fact, the clandestine grave suggests removal or distancing from society's bounds, situating a body in a place not governed by society's rules, that is, 'wild'.

We see that the opportunity to 'lay to rest' is important to those people with firm social links to the dead. The strong movement to repatriate dead remains by indigenous communities all over the world demonstrates how ideas about treatment of the dead become sharpened against noncustomary circumstances. Reconstituting the grave through reburial is a means of reordering a situation.

The Importance of Body Recovery

The object of a clandestine burial, the corpse (once a human being), represents different things to different people. It is a linkage to the murderer and a source of exposure to a crime, it is a lost 'loved one' to someone, it is a representation of tragic possibilities to others, and for the investigators it is the target of casework. The body buried in a clandestine grave becomes a source of evidence to be located and uncovered. It allows for a contemporary reconstruction of events that is seen as a source of truth. The body enables the identity of the victim to be established, is a source of scientific information (considered objective) and becomes a significant tool in the judicial process. At this point, the forensic anthropologists and pathologists are the interpreters of what the body has to convey (Crossland, 2009).

Although the body has no economic value, it has high emotional value. The body must be found to 'rebury'. In an unmarked grave, there is the risk of the remains being disturbed or desecrated at some later point. For the family of the victim, there is the need to locate the body to provide 'proper burial'. This is the expressed desire of relatives of unfound murder victims, such as continues to be for the mother of young Keith Bennet, a Saddleworth Moor murder victim in the United Kingdom (in 1964). We may also be reminded of the long-running search for the missing Beaumont children of South Australia, who disappeared in 1966.

The Effect of a Clandestine Grave on Society

The clandestine grave, when made known to the public through the media, by its very existence has implications for the wider society. As an event, it must either be ignored or somehow incorporated into explicable terms. We are dependent on the media for the transmission of such events in a timely way. The frequency of these incidents is never stated (compare, for example, with the publicity of road deaths or annual homicide figures). Fleming (2007) gives as an example that there are approximately four mass murders per month in the United States, but news items tend to be geographically isolated (reported locally) unless there are other key factors, such as multiple victims, child murders or strange methods of body disposal.

Although it is an individual that dies, and not known to most in larger contemporary cities, the clandestine grave generates a shared social concern; that of 'tribe survival', for rules have been broken and the social fabric jarred. The social response, channelled through the responsible agencies, is to restore order. There are three levels at which this social fabric must be restored. First, without a body, a person remains missing rather than dead. Second, until the grave is located, customary exequies cannot be enacted. The more time that passes before a clandestine grave is found, the more the body will decay and alter in appearance. Third, the perpetrator must be identified and taken through the judicial process.

The discovery or prospect of a clandestine grave suggests inherent danger and the prospect of repetition. Consider how the figure of the perpetrator is presented after the discovery of the clandestine grave. The murderer is credited with a capacity for malicious violence that poses a threat to the social order. Murder is not perceived as a 'contagion', but it is isolated to an individual (or group of perpetrators) who has transgressed the social order. Transgressing the law is dangerous and suggestive of a source of power; the power to disregard everyday rules. Use of such powers is threatening and Douglas refers to such persons as malefactors, who must be sought out and whose victims are innocent (1966). To reduce the risk to others, the threat of violence must be physically removed from the community (vaulted in a prison).

This potential power, or impression of being unconfined by rules of behaviour, is undermined by the attribution of a deficiency framed in medical terms. Experts describe criminals using terms that generate stereotypes, for example, *psychopathy, anomie, undersocialisation* and others (Swigert & Farrell, 1976). Palmer (1960), in a study of murderers, links exposure to severe early frustration to undersocialisation, suggesting that although murderers may display an appearance of being socialised, they presume an element of repressed aggression. This type of approach enhances the idea of a mystique of the appearance of normality that masks underlying sociopathy. There are no external 'markers' to identify this person who might be one's neighbour or co-worker.

A murder needs to be explained in order to quash fears or to restrict 'doubts about the adequacy of social arrangements to prevent death' (Aries, 1974, p. 134). To restore a sense of order, the focus has been on solving the case, rather than considering more closely the nature of the act. This is consistent with attributing significance and potency to forensic science in crimes. For example, one response has been to publicise information about highly technological instruments that 'detect' bodies. Despite this, most bodies are found inadvertently, as we saw from earlier data sources. An archaeologist in the United Kingdom, who had at the time been involved in 20–30 location cases, could not recall a single successful case that used geophysical instruments (personal communication, 2001). This is not to say they are not useful and lead to successful locations, but rather that there is a set of unrealistic expectations placed on currently available technology for this purpose. Television programs and novels that portray such instruments as a quick and reliable detection method certainly make for better television than is the reality.

The clandestine grave is a breach in orderly expectations. These breaches are that:

- a death has been caused by another
- there has been an attempt to hide the body and subvert this act coming to light
- the perpetrator has continued on with life having committed a serious crime
- the acknowledgment of a death and funereal practices have been prevented for the victim
- the victim has been removed from society in life and death.

We do not know this has occurred until the body is located. Customary behaviour — the burial of a body — takes place in a noncustomary setting. Explanatory focus is centred on the dysfunctional perpetrator, who is not easily identifiable in society. The clandestine grave itself is a post-act indicator.

By and large, communities such as urban contemporary Australia are secular. An interesting direction to explore is to consider those social contexts or societies in which bodies are not hidden. For example, is secularisation of society a key factor?

Relating Cultural Factors to the Search for Clandestine Graves

This chapter has been the first step towards examining the human activity of burying the bodies of persons killed by others. The aim has been to explore the cultural bases, possible props and prompts to this action, and could not in this space be comprehensive.

The decision by the perpetrator to move a body from a crime scene to another place severs links to the crime scene. The clandestine grave conceals and displaces the body. Although the body is hidden within a grave, the grave may be quite shallow or even simply comprise a covering of landscape-based matter (such as leaves and logs). This suggests that there is no intention to preserve the body and decomposition is either desired or at least not inhibited.

The majority of bodies found in such graves are mostly in areas that may be characterised as not closely tended. That is, the landscape is for passive engagement, such as areas set aside for walking and preserving the area for scenic purposes. Rather, they are areas not likely to be excavated at the time of burial. Private backyards, in which burials have been found, are within the control of the perpetrator and of course, if found, pose a higher risk of linking the body with the owner.

For those burials found, it seems that the locations reflect transport of the body in a car and minimal carrying of the body from points of road access. In scrubland areas or national parks, there is likely to be more difficulty in associating the perpetrator with the act. Until the body is found, the victim remains missing rather than presumed dead. Clandestine burials in 'unused' areas are also likely to be discovered by rodents and scavenging animals, which will increase the likelihood of bones being found in the vicinity.

Although there are other methods of body disposal and variations to the clandestine grave (such as the separate burial of body parts), shallow burial has continued to be used to conceal murder victims. It is the reflection of normative practice transposed to suit different motives.

8

Constructing a Search for a Clandestine Grave

A systematic series of stages ensures a well-prepared and well-informed investigative search for a clandestine grave. It does not guarantee the success of a single search, but it will eliminate many sources of potential oversight and allows for extended searching on a firm basis. There are two phases in the framework described here; a preparation phase (Phase 1) and the search phase itself (Phase 2). The framework builds on search stages proposed by Killam (1990), Dirkmaat and Adovasio (1997) and the work of Necrosearch (personal communication, September, 2001).

Phase 1: Collation of Search Related Data

Thorough preparation that includes assimilating and critically assessing information gives a solid basis for considering the outcomes of any unsuccessful site searches in order to better position the focus of subsequent searches. It is unrealistic to find the target in one search.

The following steps and considerations should be included in the first phase of any investigative search for a grave:

1. Discuss with the police the available information that can be disclosed to assist in identifying a broad locale for the deposition of the subject body. The information will include any witness accounts, verbal disclosures, and background information on suspects. If the initiator of the search is not a police officer, ensure the police are informed and permission to search is obtained. This is because the investigator is dealing with a potential crime scene.

2. Ascertain any preliminary search areas that may have been targeted already and the reasons for this. Include revision of areas already searched and why they may have been discounted.

3. Assess the limitations of knowledge, the reliability of known data and identify possible sources of error (such as mistakes in the direction of travel, ambiguous landmarks and confusion in estimating distance when areas are earmarked based on verbal accounts). This will assist in identifying alternative search areas later during the search process if no potential target areas are found.

4. Estimate the length of time since suspected interment. This assists in assessing the degree of decomposition and likely surface indicators of a gravesite.

5. Obtain maps of the suspected search area(s). These should include a topographical map and road map. Cadastral boundaries are useful to identify private and public land and associated permissions for entry. Consideration should also be given to the possibility of Indigenous and other heritage sites particular to a country.

6. Outline the broadest possible area for searching based on what is known to date. Outline the most likely area within this to prioritise when on site. This can be modified as further information is incorporated into the search file.

7. If available, obtain aerial photographs of area (preferably including pre and postburial). These will provide topographical information to complement the maps, such as buildings in the area. They may also indicate relevant changes to the area since the estimated time of burial.

8. From the maps and any other topographical data obtained, note the nature of the landscape (rocky, tree covered, degree vegetation, soil type, undulation, uniformity) and the layout of trees, shrubs, logs and features that would be either natural obstacles to digging or would provide useful camouflages. Consider any changes that could have occurred since estimated interment that may influence the selection of areas to search in depth or mask a burial site, such as excavation, cropping or building. This will also help to determine the usefulness or limitations of any geophysical instruments used.

9. Determine road access and the distance the body would be likely to have been either transported by vehicle or carried in the target areas. This may narrow the search area.

10. Obtain any available data on the soil type or range of soil types and underlying surface. For example, if there is solid bedrock beneath the surface it may indicate the potential likelihood of a shallow burial or an unlikely place for a burial. A geologist or relevant government department is a useful source of this information.

11. Attempt to establish the season of burial (which may have some bearing on level of vegetation at the time of burial).

12. Consider local climatic conditions, especially recent weather conditions, as this will influence the degree of vegetation regrowth over the burial site.

13. Identify the fauna within the area, for likely indications of scavenging and rodent activity.

14. Obtain any necessary permissions to enter the targeted properties (whether private, conservation parks or such) and conduct excavations.

Phase 2: Field Search and the Identification of Likely Surface Anomalies

1. Select an optimal season for search that will maximise surface visibility (choice in this matter will depend on the degree of urgency and the circumstances of the case). Interim seasons (spring or autumn) or summer maximises ground visibility due to minimal vegetation.

2. Once at the site, 2–3 holes should be dug into the ground (approximately 0.5–1 m) within the search area to identify the likely colour and texture of upcast soil. If years have passed since the burial, there may have been some fading of the upcast due to surface exposure. The holes will give an indication of the variability of the stratigraphy within the search zone.

3. Undertake a sample ground survey of the search zone(s) of a smaller area. Examine the vegetation patterns and surface texture closely. The purpose of this is to accustom the searcher to recognise what is usual in the area and to be able to identify during the search proper what may be anomalous. Binoculars can be useful magnifiers of the surface. It is recommended that a ground search be conducted twice over the same area for this reason.

4. It is important to describe what is likely to be a surface anomaly in the area for those persons assisting in a search. Potential gravesites will be of a relatively small size. A grave is a small, defined area within a landscape, and is unlikely to be located from a distance. As such, indicators of a grave will all be found within the immediate grave environment;

within a 1–3 m radius from the grave itself. The following surface signs will earmark potential sites and will be based on the surface and sub-surface geology and topography of the target area:

- change in the colour of the soil, indicating upcast
- change in the texture of the surface soil (softness, cracking)
- lack of surface debris (ground litter) if this is otherwise characteristic of the area
- signs of scavenging, such as burrows (and possibly bones lying on the surface)
- animal burrows that may have been made over a gravesite and are now faunal habitats
- sparser vegetation over the upcast area or more fast growing weeds growing in one area (identify likely succession plants);
- depending on estimated length of time since burial, consider surrounding vegetation growth
- a noticeable halo of little or no vegetation and cracked ground if it is a summer period
- traversing tracks (flattened grass, vehicle tracks)
- shallow dips to the surface, including those that have vegetation growing within the dips (these may be depressions due to the body or evidence of burrowing)
- absence of moss if it occurs within the area (depending on season of search). This is not a reliable or key indicator in itself.

5. The search itself should be approached methodically to ensure all areas are surveyed. The method used will depend on how many foot searchers may be available to assist (who should be briefed as to likely indicators) and the nature of the terrain. Methods of foot surveys are: marking out laneways for each walker and snaking forwards (in 's' movements) within each single laneway; emu walking forwards in a line; marking out large square grids and allocating a responsible person for each grid; spacing people over an area and walking in ever-widening concentric circles from the starting point; having two rows of people at opposite ends of a square area walking towards each other in an emu walk (this helps to minimise signs being missed because the same area is surveyed twice); and continuing past each other to effectively traverse the same area twice but with different eyes. During the search, nothing should be picked up, if possible, from the ground (see use of markers below).

6. Mark by noninvasive means identified possible sites (either because of visual signs or because of convenience for burial, or any other reason, as they can always be eliminated when re-examined later). This can be done by ribbons tied to trees or shrubs, or by tent pegs with colour flags. Waterproof plastic markers are best as they can be left there if the search is not completed in one day.

7. Re-examine each of the marked sites. Preliminary excavation may be carried out. A soil probe or trowel (to ascertain if upcast is on the near surface) could be carefully used at each of the sites to assist in this process. A ground probe could be included during this phase. The purpose of the preliminary excavation is to reduce the number of search sites. It may be done by surface scraping the topsoil to ascertain subsurface soil disturbance, using a trowel in a manner to ensure there is no damage to any bones. A comparison hole nearby can be dug to provide an indication of adjacent soil horizons and clearly show any differences indicative of prior disturbance.

8. Once the number of potential gravesites has been decreased, further examination may proceed by either careful excavation to a deeper level or by applying subsurface detection methods. Careful excavation will quickly confirm the presence of upcast or prior disturbance.

9. The decision as to whether to use subsurface geophysical instruments will be influenced by resources available to the investigators and the practicality of disturbing the area through excavations.

Subsurface detection methods

If subsurface or remote sensing instruments are incorporated into the search strategy, an instrument or instruments will need to be selected. The ground search stage should have revealed areas that may be prioritised. Where the area is such that surface signs are clearly identified, such as very sandy areas with little vegetation, subsurface instruments may be a practical alternative.

The steps involved in incorporating subsurface geophysical instruments into the search are described.

1. Identify the instrument most likely to yield useful results under the circumstances (including terrain type, subsurface root systems and previous buried debris, climatic conditions, soil type, approximated depth of burial and sources of interference to the instrument). The nature of the terrain will provide some parameters for the type of instrument best able to be applied. More than one instrument is more likely to result in some confirmation of a possible burial.

2. Clear the area as far as possible of surface vegetation, large rocks and any metal objects, providing permissions have been obtained to do this.

3. Conduct an instrument orientation survey.

4. Proceed with the surveys and examine the flagged areas.

5. Determine if excavation can follow, based on an examination of the date, with appropriate permissions.

Excavating the gravesite

Whichever method is used to detect a clandestine grave, the final phase will be excavation and recovery. Excavation will always be the means whereby the remains will be recovered, and may also be the means whereby the subsurface instrument results are confirmed or found to be indicative of something else.

A portable grid method is shown in the photograph in Figure 8.1 of a teaching excavation exercise.

The most appropriate method of excavation is archaeologically based, because the aim in a criminal investigation is to preserve and audit evidence that may be critical to the judicial process. Excavation should be

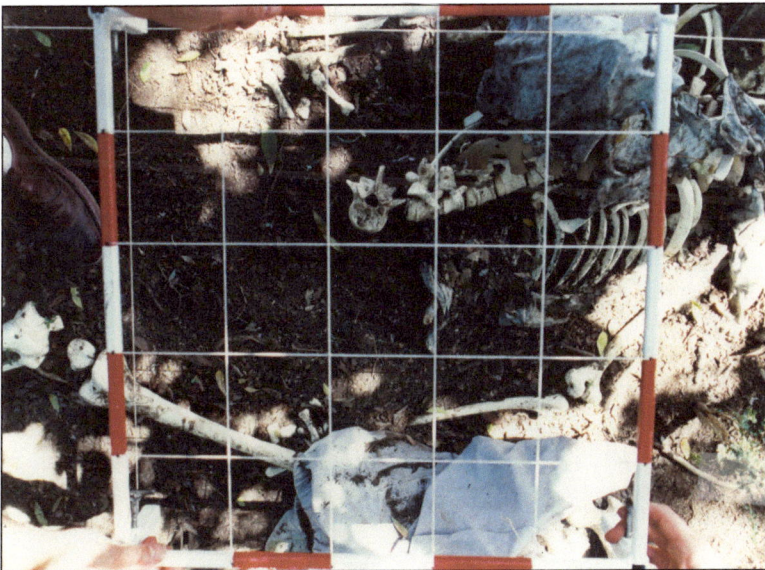

FIGURE 8.1
Portable grid overlay.
(Source: SA Police, published with permission.

carefully structured to allow documentation of the location and position of all objects found within and nearby the grave. The key steps may be summarised for these purposes:

1. Mark off the area with tape and plot a grid system that will allow the transfer of all finds to be clearly marked on a paper map.

2. Excavate thin layers from the surface to identify the shape and size of the grave. This will be seen by the colour changes of the soil, indicating the line of shovelling or demarcation between disturbed and undisturbed soil.

3. Tools that will not endanger the preservation of skeletal material should be used, and professionals in the anthropological and archaeological fields will employ these.

4. As much of the surrounding soil of any bodies located as possible should be bagged for sieving later.

5. All steps should be photographed and each bone should be photographed in situ with accompanying scale indicators.

6. All bones should be placed in suitable packing and containers to prevent damage during transportation, labelling these with place of grid location and depth. Police will direct that the grave contents be transported to a forensic examination laboratory.

Conclusion

Evidence exists for the deliberate disposals of dead people after approximately 100,000 years ago. This book has considered a particular type of deliberate body disposal in contemporary times. This is the hidden burial, *krupton* (Greek for hidden) or clandestine grave, which is not characterised by commonly observed funeral practices. Although the death may be unintended, a clandestine grave is never created inadvertently or accidentally. The information contained in this book is organised to address two main questions: what do we know about clandestine graves, and how do we go about locating the bodies buried within? To answer these questions, we have examined the physical landscape of the burial and the cultural landscape in which it transpires.

In the physical landscape, the body of the victim will almost certainly remain within the burial without completely deteriorating, because we are dealing with relatively recent events compared with historical burials. No matter if it is some years after death, and even if decomposition is extensive, the bones at least are most likely to remain to be found. This is an advantage of the crime scene burial compared with the historical burial.

As clandestine graves necessarily result from, and are in themselves, criminal activities, police play a key role in the investigation process. The physical location is generally defined by police first. The process of grave location and the development of search techniques have been moderated by police to the extent their development has been somewhat contingent on police willingness to engage forensic expertise. When this more frequently occurred, from the 1980s especially, research was generated. It is still not always the case that police engage such expertise, such that during cases there will often have been areas searched via the digging of 'potholes' by police teams before expert advice is sought. This is part of the reality of investigations that are indeed the domain of police, and buried human remains are not always approached in a methodical or ideal manner. It is also part of the developing nature of searching for hidden body disposals, and the interface between policing and science.

In terms of the practices and research associated with burials that can be applied to clandestine or unmarked graves, the desire of indigenous peoples around the world to repatriate human remains has played a part in somewhat limiting burial site work. Previously, this work provided impetus for research on burials and their detection.

Buried human remains have been the subject of varied search techniques, which have been based on above- and below-ground landscape features. These features are the result of the creation of a burial, and not only the interment of a human body. For example, the surface landscape is changed through the act of digging a hole and refilling it. Where a body might be buried involves scanning the landscape and marking out features that can be associated with an inhumation, and it is important to be inclusive rather than exclusive of potential features. It is much simpler to mark out potential burial sites in areas that are seldom areas of activity compared with areas that are frequented by people. In most areas, there is a high potential for bones scavenged by animals to be in close proximity on the surface close to a gravesite. In cases of dismemberment and the separate burial of body parts, the death of an individual cannot always be assumed.

Below ground, the body within the earth is a site of extensive transformation as the body decomposes under the influence of external conditions. Principal changes relevant to the location of gravesites here are those that relate to the altered subsurface structure of the soil and its properties. In order to better detect buried human remains, approaches should be based on the identification of specific indicators associated with graves. Some grave identifiers will be subtle, but several in combination will serve to mark an area for preliminary excavation.

There is, however, relative few research studies about buried remains and the enduring below-surface characteristics that might be applied to search principles. Understanding the nature of these transformations will contribute to determining the best methods of detecting distinctions within the landscape that are indicative of possible buried human remains.

There are differences between scanning the above burial signs and the below-ground surface signs. Most of the signs are relatively subtle, unless the grave is relatively recent. Geophysical instruments certainly have an allure and promise to locate the hidden body beneath the earth, although for this purpose, their current capacity to detect single human burials without coffins is probably overstated. Landscapes that seem to be favoured for clandestine graves are not always conducive to yielding the best results for most geophysical instruments suitable for this purpose.

Scanning below surface entails the identification of areas of soil aeration and stratigraphic interference. Ideally, larger subsurface objects can be demarcated, but distinguishing the detail of such objects can mean several false positives, such as rocks, tree roots and man-made debris, will be captured. The simple fact is that subsurface technology has been developed for much greater depths than the shallow-buried murder victim, and is not designed to detect the relatively subtle subsurface differences. Having emphasised some caution, it is important to recognise the potential this technology offers, and realise that this potential lies in refining the application of some instruments and technological principles to this purpose, and with the more common burial landscape features in mind.

The hiding of a body occurs regularly in contemporary societies. The burial of murder victims in clandestine graves is sufficiently embedded in the contemporary societies of their incidence, to the extent that it is a recurring practice. At two levels it is explicitly not condoned, and is in fact, outlawed. The first level is that the death has not been reported, and the second, that the body has been the object of interference. Further, the burial has occurred in a nondesignated place. The ongoing incidence of body disposals in this way suggests that contemporary living lends some degree of support to this behaviour or is, in some manner, channelling this behaviour. Bearing in mind the limitations on direct research on body disposal and those who do this, we have been able to explore the cultural landscape and identify elements of a cultural basis for the burial of murder victims. In terms of the cultural context in which the clandestine grave is enacted, we assume concealment of the body (representing a serious crime) is paramount. Disposal of the body may also constitute a diversionary or deflective activity, creating a distance between the perpetrator and the crime. It also distances the victim from association with their fate because for others, until the point of body discovery, they are considered missing. As a practice, it is not confined to serial killers, but is undertaken by persons who have taken a life for the first time, and further, it does not appear to be restricted to demarcated sections of society (e.g., the practice of a mafia type group). The individuals who commit this act are not portrayed as especially distinctive after discovery; persons who bury bodies are not mad, insane or attributed with a disease. This is not to say retrospective explanations do not attribute a form of malfunctioning to the perpetrator, but rather such persons are not readily identifiable within the community and the behaviour is not seen as being able to be predicted, even if explanations are formulated later.

This brief venture into the cultural landscape of clandestine graves opens up issues for further anthropological study, such as the cross-cultural incidence (or absence) of this act, and the incidence within identifiable community segments.

There is a Gaelic phrase 'uaigh a' choigrich', meaning the grave of the stranger. Such are clandestine graves, unmarked resting places of strangers to most. These wait to be uncovered and for their remains to testify the events that brought them there. When found, the grave and the body are forensic keys to resolving a crime. The place of deposit will not be marked, noted or signed in any way (compared with roadside death markers).

At first, the task of locating a single unmarked grave may appear insurmountable. Locating a buried body can be achieved through the careful scrutiny of both the physical and cultural aspects of the clandestine grave. The location process is dependent on putting together enough information to identify a target area after the disappearance of someone and accompanied by astute police suspicion of foul play. Scrubland areas are not intermittently scoured as possible burial sites, even though enough bodies are found in such areas to perhaps justify this activity periodically, including holding photographic records.

Issues of more immediate concern that can be readily taken up are the collection of information relating to the characteristics of clandestine graves, such as the location of graves found in relation to the death scene, distance from the perpetrator's home, time delay from death to burial and reasons why perpetrators select certain places for body disposal.

This book has sought to describe and explain clandestine graves. There is a broader area now to explore as a modern phenomenon, and that is the many other ways in which bodies are disposed of after a crime, and as a form of crime. As we saw briefly, the physical and cultural landscape sadly provides opportunities for inventive ways to dispose of bodies.

References

Allanson, A. (2004). Soursob; Sour by name, sour by nature and souring our bushland. *Releaf, June.* Adelaide, Australia: Trees for Life.

Aries, P. (1974). *Western attitudes towards death: From the middle ages to the present.* Baltimore, MD: The John Hopkins University Press.

Aturaliya, S., & Lukasewycz, A. (1999). Experimental forensic and bioanthropological aspects of soft tissue taphonomy: 1. Factors influencing postmortem tissue dessication rate. *Journal of Forensic Sciences, 44*(5), 893–896.

Australian Institute of Criminology. (2005). *Crime facts info.* (No. 108). Canberra, Australia: Australian Institute of Criminology.

Awofeso, N. (2003). Burial rituals as noble lies — an Australian perspective. *Journal of Mundane Behaviour,* May 2003. Retrieved July 2, 2008 from http://mundanebehaviour.org/issues/v4n1/awofeso4-1.html

Bass, W. (1987). Forensic anthropology: The American experience. In A. Boddington, A.N. Garland & R.C. Janaway (Eds.), *Death, decay and reconstruction: Approaches to archaeology and forensic science* (pp. 224–239). Manchester: Manchester University Press.

Bass, W. (1997). Outdoor decomposition rates in tennessee. In W.D. Haglund & M.H. Sorg (Eds.), *Forensic taphonomy: The postmortem fate of human remains* (pp. 181–186). New York: CRC Press.

Beck, L.A. (1982). Anthropology and criminal forensics — A growing alliance. *Criminal Justice Review, 7*(1), 1–10.

Bell, L.S., Skinner, M., & Jones, S.J. (1996). The speed of post mortem change to the human skeleton and its taphonomic significance. *Forensic Science International, 82,* 129–140.

Bethell, P.H., & Carver, M.O.H. (1987). Detection and enhancement of decayed inhumations at Sutton Hoo. In A. Boddington, A.N. Garland & R.C. Janaway (Eds.), *Death, decay and reconstruction: Approaches to archaeology and forensic science* (pp. 10–21). Manchester: Manchester University Press.

Bevan, B.W. (1991). The search for graves. *Geophysics, 56*(9), 1310–1319.

Binford, L.R. (1981). *Bones: Ancient men and modern myths.* New York: Academic Press.

Bock, J.H., & Norris, D.O. (1997). Forensic botany: An under-utilized resource. *Journal of Forensic Sciences, 42*(3), 364–347.

Boddington, A., Garland, A.N., & Janaway, R.C. (Eds.) (1987). *Death, decay and reconstruction: Approaches to archaeology and forensic science.* Manchester, UK: Manchester University Press.

Bossard, A., & Negrier-Dormont, L. (2000). Profiling serial killers. *International Crime Police Review. 481*, 25–29.

Boyd, R.M. (1979). Buried body cases. *FBI Law Enforcement Bulletin, 48*(2), 1–6.

Bradbury, M. (1999). *Representations of death: A social psychological perspective.* London: Routledge.

Brothwell, D.R. (1965). *Digging up bones: The excavation, treatment and study of human skeletal remains.* London: William Clowes & Sons Limited.

Buck, S.C. (2003). Searching for graves using geophysical technology: Field tests with ground penetrating radar, magnetometry, and electrical resistivity. *Journal of Forensic Sciences, 48*(1), 5–11.

Burnside, J. (2007). *The devil's footprints.* London: Random House.

Burton, J.A., Price, T.D., Cahue, L., & Wright, L.E. (2003). The use of barium and strontium abundances in human skeletal tissues to determine their geographic origins. *International Journal of Osteoarchaeology, 13*, 88–95.

Butzer, K.W. (1982). *Archaeology as human ecology: Method and theory for a contextual approach.* New York: Cambridge University Press.

Byers, S.N. (2002). *Introduction to Forensic Anthropology.* Boston: Allyn & Bacon.

Carter, D.O., & Tibbett, M. (2003). Taphonomic Mycota: Fungi with Forensic Potential. *Journal of Forensic Sciences, 48*(1), 168–171.

Carter, D.O., Yellowlees, D., & Tibbett, M. (2008). Using ninhydrin to detect gravesoil. *Journal of Forensic Sciences, 53*(2), 397–400.

Chamberlain, A. (1994). *Interpreting the past: Human remains.* London: British Museum Press.

Chamberlain, A.T., & Pearson, M.P. (2001). *Earthly remains: The history and science of preserved human bodies.* London: British Museum Press.

Chapman, R. (1987). Mortuary Practices: Society, Theory Building and Archaeology. In A. Boddington, A.N. Garland, & R.C. Janaway (Eds.), *Death, decay and reconstruction: Approaches to archaeology and forensic science* (pp. 198–216). Manchester: Manchester University Press.

Charmaz, K., Howarth, G., & Kellehear, A. (Eds.) (1997). *The unknown country: Death in Australia. Britain and the USA.* London: Macmillan Press Limited.

Child, A.M. *(1995).* Towards an understanding of the microbial decomposition of archaeological bone in the burial environment. *Journal of Archaeological Science, 22*, 165–174.

Cockroft, B., & Martin, F.M. (1981). Irrigation. In J.M. Oades, D.G. Lewis & K. Norrish (Eds.), *Red-brown earths of Australia,* (pp. 133–148). Adelaide: Waite Agricultural Research Institute, University of Adelaide and the Commonwealth Scientific and Industrial Research Organisation Division of Soils.

Coleman, P. (1997). *Corpses, coffins, and crypts: a history of burial.* New York: Henry Holt & Company.

Collier, C.D. Abby (2003). Tradition, modernity, and postmodernity in symbolism of death. *Sociological Quarterly, 44*(4), 727–749.

Collins, M., Nielson-Marsh, C.M., Hiller, J., Smith, C.I., & Roberts, J.P. (2002). The survival of organic matter in bone. *Archaeometry, 44*(3), 383–394.

Cox, M., & Bell, L. (1999). Recovery of human skeletal elements from a recent UK murder inquiry: Preservational signatures. *Journal of Forensic Sciences, 44*(5), 945–950.

Crooks, M. (2005, January). Conversations with a killer. *Who,* pp. 50–52.

Crossland, Z. (2009). Of clues and signs: The dead body and its evidential traces. *American Anthropologist, 111*(1), 69–80.

Davenport, G.C. (2001). Remote sensing applications in forensic investigations. *Historical Archaeology, 35*(1), 87–100.

David, A., & Linford, N. (2000). Physics and archaeology. *Physics World, May,* 27–31.

Davis, J.L., Heginbottom, J.A., Anman, A.P., Daniels, R.S., Berdal, B.P., Bergan, T., et al. (2000). Ground penetrating radar surveys to locate 1918 Spanish flu victims in permafrost. *Journal of Forensic Sciences, 45*(1), 68–76.

Dearden, J., & Jones, W. (2008). *Homicide in Australia: 2006–07 National Homicide Monitoring Program Annual Report.* Canberra, Australia: Australian Institute of Criminology.

Department of Environment and Heritage. (2003). *State of the Environment Report for South Australia: Supplementary report.* Adelaide, South Australia: Department of Environment and Heritage.

Dirkmaat, D.C., & Adovasio, J.M. (1997). The role of archaeology in the recovery and interpretation of human remains from an outdoor forensic setting. In W.D. Haglund & M.H. Sorg (Eds.), *Forensic taphonomy: The postmortem fate of human remains* (pp. 39–64). New York: CRC Press.

Douglas, M. (1966). *Purity and danger.* London: Penguin Books.

Duncan, J. (1983). Search techniques. In D. Morse, J. Duncan & J. Stoutamire (Eds.), *Handbook of Forensic Archaeology and Anthropology,* (pp. 4–19). Tallahassee, FL: Florida State University Foundation.

Ebert, J.I. (1984). Remote sensing applications in archaeology. In M.B. Schiffer (Ed.), *Advances in archaeological method and theory* (Vol. 7, pp. 293–361). Gainesville, FL: Academic Press.

Edward, J.B., & Benfer, R.A. (1993). The effects of diagenesis on the Paloma skeletal material. In M. Sandford (Ed.), *Investigations of ancient human tissue: Chemical analyses in anthropology* (pp. 178–268). Pennsylvania: Gordon & Breach Science Publishers.

Eldridge, D.J., & Kinnell, P.I.A. (1997). Assessment of erosion rates from microphyte-dominated calcareous soils under rain-impacted flow. *Australian Journal of Soil Research, 32,* 475–489.

Emsley, J. (1991). *The elements,* (2nd ed.). Oxford: Clarendon.

Evans, W.E.D. (1963). *The chemistry of death.* Springfield, IL: Charles C. Thomas.

Fifth Australasian Remote Sensing Conference Proceedings. (1990). Perth, Western Australia, October 8–12, 1990.

Fischer, P.M. (1980). Applications of technical devices in archaeology: The use of x-rays, electrical and electro-magnetic devices and subsurface interface radar. In P. Astroms Forlag (Ed.), *Studies in Mediterranean Archaeology Volume LX111,* Goteborg, Sweden.

Fitzpatrick, L. (1997). Secular, Savage and Solitary: Death in Australian Painting. In K. Charmaz, G. Howarth & A. Kellehear (Eds.), *The unknown country: Death in Australia, Britain and the USA* (pp. 1–14). London: Macmillan Press Limited.

Fleming, T. (2007). The history of violence: Mega cases of serial murder, self-propelling narratives, and reader engagement. *Journal of Criminal Justice and Popular Culture, 14*(3), 277–291.

France, D.L., Griffin, T.J., Swanburg, J.G., Lindeman, J.W., Davenport, G.C., Trammell, V., Armhurst, C.T., Kondratieff, B., Nelson, A., Castellano, K., & Hopkins, D. (1992). A Multidisciplinary approach to the detection of clandestine graves. *Journal of Forensic Sciences, 37*(6), 1445–1458.

France, D.L., Griffin, T.J., Swanburg, J.G., Lindeman, J.W., Davenport, G.C., Trammell, V., Travis, C., Kondratieff, B., Nelson, A., Castellano, K., Hopkins, D., & Adair, T. (1997). Necrosearch revisited: Further multidisciplinary approaches to the detection of clandestine graves. In W.D. Haglund & M.H. Sorg (Eds.), *Forensic taphonomy: The postmortem fate of human remains* (pp. 497–509). New York: CRC Press.

Frazier, C.H., Cadalli, N., Munson Jnr, D.C., & O'Brien, W.D. (2000). Acoustic imaging of objects buried in soil. *Journal of the Acoustical Society of America, 108*(1), 147–156.

Freeland, R.S., Miller, M.L., Yoder, R.E., & Koppenjan, S.K. (2003). Forensic application of FM-CW and pulse radar. *Journal of Environmental and Engineering Geophysics, June*(2), 97–108.

French, R.J. (1981). Management under low rainfall: South Australia. In J.M. Oades, D.G Lewis & K. Norrish (Eds.), *Red-brown earths of Australia*, (pp. 97–116). Adelaide, Australia: Waite Agricultural Research Institute, University of Adelaide and the Commonwealth Scientific and Industrial Research Organisation Division of Soils.

Galloway, A., Birkby, W.H., Jones, A.M., Henry, T.E., & Parks, B. (1989). Decay rates of human remains in an arid environment. *Australian Journal of Forensic Sciences, 34*, 607–616.

Garland, A.N. (1987). A histological study of archaeological bone decomposition. In A. Boddington, A.N. Garland & R.C. Janaway (Eds.), *Death, decay and reconstruction: Approaches to archaeology and forensic science* (pp. 109–126). Manchester, UK: Manchester University Press.

Garland, A.N., & Janaway, R.C. (1989). The taphonomy of inhumation burials. In C.A. Roberts, F. Lee & J. Bintiff (Eds.), *Burial archaeology: Current research, methods and developments* (pp. 15–37). Oxford: BAR British Series 211.

Geberth, V.J. (1983). *Practical homicide investigation: Tactics, procedures, and forensic techniques.* New York: Elsevier.

Gibbon, G. (1939). *Anthropological archaeology.* (1984 ed.). New York: Columbia University Press.

Glaskin, K., Tonkinson, M., Musharbash, Y., & Burbank, V. (2008). *Mortality, mourning and mortuary practices in Indigenous Australia.* Surrey, UK: Ashgate Publishing Company.

Godwin, M., & Canter, D. (1997). Encounter and death: The spatial behaviour of us serial killers. *Policing: An International Journal of Police Strategy and Management, 20*(1), 24–38.

Goffer, Z. (1980). *Archaeological chemistry: A source book on the applications of chemistry to archaeology.* New York: Wiley.

Gray, H. (author), Williams, P.L., Bannister, L.H., Berry, M.M., Collins, P., Dyson, M., Dussek, J.E., & Ferguson, M.W.J. (Eds.). (1995). *Gray's anatomy* (38th ed.). Edinburgh: Churchill Livingstone.

Haglund, W.D., & Sorg, M.H. (1997). Method and theory of forensic taphonomic research. In W.D. Haglund & M.H. Sorg (Eds.), *Forensic taphonomy: The postmortem fate of human remains* (pp. 13–26). New York: CRC Press.

Haglund, W.D., & Sorg, M.H. (Eds.) (1997). *Forensic taphonomy: The postmortem fate of human remains.* New York: CRC Press.

Haglund, W.D. (1997). Dogs and Coyotes: Postmortem Involvement with Human Remains. In W.D. Haglund & M.H. Sorg (Eds.), *Forensic taphonomy: The postmortem fate of human remains*, (pp. 367–381). New York: CRC Press.

Hammon III, W.S., McMechan, G.A., & Zeng, X. (2000). Forensic GPR: Finite-difference simulations of responses from buried human remains. *Journal of Applied Geophysics, 45*, 171–186.

Hardesty, D.L. (1941). *Ecological anthropology.* New York: John Wiley & Sons.

Haviland, W.A. (1987). *Cultural Anthropology* (5th ed.). New York: Holt, Rinehart & Winston, Inc.

Hays, W.M. (2008). *Florida's clandestine graves: An anthropological perspective of the dead.* Unpublished Masters Thesis, Florida State University, FL.

Healing, T.D., Hoffman, P.N., & Young, S.E.J. (1995). The infection hazards of human cadavers. *Communicable Disease Report, 5*(5), 2R61–R68.

Hedges, R.E.M. (2002). Bone diagenesis: An overview of processes. *Archaeometry, 44*(3), 319–328.

Henderson, J. (1987). Factors determining the state of preservation of human remains. In A. Boddington, A.N. Garland, & R.C. Janaway (Eds.), *Death, decay and reconstruction: approaches to archaeology and forensic science* (pp. 43–54). Manchester: Manchester University Press.

Henderson, M., Henderson, P., & Keirnan, C. (2000). Missing persons: Incidence, issues and impacts. *Trends and Issues in Crime and Criminal Justice* (No. 144). Canberra, Australia: Australian Institute of Criminology.

Heizer, R.F. (Ed.). (1959). *The archaeologist at work: A source book in archaeological method and interpretation.* New York: Harper & Brothers.

Hoffman, E.M., Curran, A.M., Dulgerian, N., Stockham, R., & Eckenrode, B.A. (2009). Characterization of the volatile compounds present in the headspace of decomposing human remains. *Forensic Science International, 186,* (Issues 1–3), 6–13.

Hole, F., & Heizer, R.F. (1965). *An introduction to prehistoric archaeology* (3rd ed.). New York: Holt, Rinehart & Winston.

Hopkins, C. (2005). *South Australia Police 1838–2003.* (2nd ed.). Adelaide, Australia: Digital Reproductions.

Hoshower, L.M. (1998). Forensic archaeology and the need for flexible excavation strategies: a case study. *Journal of Forensic Sciences, 43*(1), 53–56.

Hoving, G. (1986). Buried body search technology. *Identification News, February*, 3–15.

Hoysted, P., & Kidd, P.B. (2002). *Shallow graves: The concealments of killers.* Melbourne, Australia: Five Mile Press.

Hunter, J. & Cox, M. (2005). *Forensic archaeology: Advances in theory and practice.* New York: Routledge.

Hunter, J., & Martin, A.L. (1996). Locating buried remains. In J. Hunter, C. Roberts & A. Martin, (Eds.), *Studies in crime: An introduction to forensic archaeology,* (pp. 88–100). London: Routledge.

Hunter, J., Roberts, C., & Martin, A. (1996). *Studies in crime: An introduction to forensic archaeology.* London: Routledge.

Imaizumi, M. (1974). Locating buried bodies. *FBI Law Enforcement Bulletin, 43*(8), 2–5.

Jalland, P. (2002). *Australian ways of death: A social and cultural history 1840–1918.* Melbourne, Australia: Oxford University Press.

Jalland, P. (2006). *Changing ways of death in twentieth century Australia: War, medicine and the funeral business.* Sydney, Australia: University of New South Wales Press, .

Janaway, R.C. (1996). The decay of buried human remains and their associated materials. In J. Hunter, C. Roberts & A. Martin, (Eds.), *Studies in crime: An introduction to forensic archaeology* (pp. 58–85). London: Routledge.

Janaway, R.C. (1987). The preservation of organic materials in association with metal artifacts deposited in inhumation graves. In A. Boddington, A.N. Garland, & R.C. Janaway (Eds.), *Death, decay and reconstruction: Approaches to archaeology and forensic science* (pp. 127–148). Manchester: Manchester University Press.

Johnson, S. (2000). *Property in human body parts extracted from living persons: A suggested approach* (Unpublished Honours thesis). University of Adelaide, Australia.

Kanable, R. (2000). Earth's clues: Outside experts and geophysical techniques help locate clandestine gravesites. *Law Enforcement Technology, 27,* 40–44.

Kearl, M.C. (1989). *Endings: A sociology of death and dying New York.* United Kingdom: Oxford University Press.

Keeley, H.C.M., Hudson, G.E., & Evans, J. (1977). Trace element contents of human bones in various states of preservation. *Journal of Archaeological Sciences, 4,* 19–24.

Kellehear, A., & Anderson, I. (1997). Death in the Country of Matilda. In K. Charmaz, G. Howarth, & A. Kellehear (Eds.), *The unknown country: Death in Australia, Britain and the USA* (pp. 1–14). London: Macmillan Press Limited.

Killam, E.W. (1990). *The detection of human remains.* Illinois: Charles C. Thomas.

Kocsis, R.N. (2000). Offender profiling in police investigations — beneficial or B.S.? *Australian Police Journal, March,* 42–46.

Kocsis, R.N. (2000). New techniques in geographic offender profiling of serial crimes. *Victoria Police Association Journal, June,* 20–23.

Komar, D.A. (1998). Decay rates in a cold climate region: A review of cases involving advanced decomposition from the Medical Examiner's Office in Edmonton, Alberta. *Journal of Forensic Sciences, 43*(1), 57–61.

Krogman, W.M. (1986). *The human skeleton in forensic medicine.* Illinois: Charles C. Thomas.

Lamp, C., & Collett, F. (1976). *A field guide to weeds in Australia.* Melbourne: Inkata Press.

Lindemann, J.W. (2000). Forensic geology: The example of professional contribution to Necrosearch International. *The Professional Geologist, 37*(9), 4–7.

Long, A., & von Strokirch, T. (2003). *Lost but not forgotten: A guide to methods of identifying Aboriginal unmarked graves.* Sydney, Australia: New South Wales National Parks & Wildlife Service.

Lord, W.D., & Goff, M. Lee, (1994). Forensic entomology: Insects in the investigation of crime. *American Journal of Forensic Medical Pathology, 15*(1), 109–117.

L'Oste-Brown, S., Goodwin, L., & Yelf, R. (1996). Taroom Aboriginal Reserve cemeteries: Their history and investigation. *Tempus, 6,* 207–218.

L'Oste-Brown, S., Godwin, L. & Morwood, M. (2002). Aboriginal bark burial: 700 years of mortuary tradition in the Central Queensland Highlands. *Australian Aboriginal Studies, 1,* 43–50.

McEwan, I. (1997). Enduring love. London: Jonathon Cape.

McGregor, D.M., Wood, W.B., & Brecknell, D.J. (1996). Soil accumulation of by-products of tissue decomposition and time since death. *Australian Journal of Forensic Sciences, 28,* 67–71.

McLaughlin, J.E. (1974). *The detection of buried bodies.* Yuba City: Andermac.

McManamon, F.P. (1984). Discovering sites unseen. In M.B. Schiffer (Ed.), *Advances in archaeological method and theory, Volume 7* (pp. 223–292). Florida: Academic Press.

Mann, R.W., Bass, W.M., & Meadows, L. (1990). Time since death and decomposition of the human body: Variables and observations in case and experimental field studies. *Journal of Forensic Sciences, 35*(1), 103–111.

Mant, A.K. (1987). Knowledge acquired from post-war exhumations. In A. Boddington, A.N. Garland & R.C. Janaway (Eds.), *Death, decay and reconstruction: approaches to archaeology and forensic science* (pp. 65–80). Manchester: Manchester University Press.

Maples, W.R., & Browning, M. (1994). *Dead men do tell tales.* London: Arrow Books.

Mellett, J.S. (1992). Location of human remains with ground penetrating radar. *Fourth International Conference on Ground Penetrating Radar,* Geological Survey of Finland, Special Paper 16, 359–65.

Metcalf, P., & Huntington, R. (1991). *Celebrations of death: The anthropology of mortuary ritual* (2nd ed.). Cambridge: Cambridge University Press.

Miller, M.L. (2002). *Coupling ground penetrating radar applications with continually changing decomposing human targets: An effort to enhance search strategies of buried human remains* (Unpublished Masters thesis). University of Tennessee, TN.

Miller, P.S. (1996). Disturbances in the soil: Finding buried bodies and other evidence using ground penetrating radar. *Journal of Forensic Sciences, 41*(4), 648–652.

Morse, D., Duncan, J., & Stoutamire, J. (Eds.) (1983). *Handbook of forensic archeology and anthropology.* Florida: Florida State University Foundation.

Murad, T.A. (1997). The utilization of faunal evidence in the recovery of human remains. In W.D. Haglund & M.H. Sorg (Eds.), *Forensic taphonomy: The postmortem fate of human remains* (pp. 395–404). New York: CRC Press.

Mykyta, A. (1980). *It's a long eay to Truro.* Melbourne, Australia: The Dominion Press.

Neubauer, W. (2001). Images of the invisible-prospection methods for the documentation of threatened archaeological sites. *Naturwissenschaften, 88,* 13–24.

New South Wales National Parks & Wildlife Service. (2003). *Lost but not forgotten: A guide to methods of identifying Aboriginal unmarked graves.* Sydney, Australia: New South Wales National Parks & Wildlife Service.

Nicol, R. (1988). *Cemeteries of South Australia: A heritage survey.* Adelaide, Australia: Department of the Environment & Planning.

Nicol, R. (1994). *At the end of the road.* Sydney, Australia: Allen & Unwin Australia.

Nobes, D.C. (1999). Geophysical surveys of burial sites: A case study of the Oaro Urupa. *Geophysics, 64*(2), 357–367.

Nobes, D.C. (2000). The search for 'Yvonne': A case example of the delineation of a grave using near-surface geophysical methods. *Journal of Forensic Sciences, 45*(3), 715–721.

Owsley, D. W. (1995). Techniques for locating burials, with emphasis on the probe. *Journal of Forensic Sciences, 40*(5), 735–740.

Palmer, S. (1960). *A Study of Murder.* New York: Thomas Y. Crowell Co.

Pate, F.D. (1997). Bone collagen diagenesis at roonka flat, south australia: implications for isotopic analysis. *Archaeology in Oceania, 32,* 170–175.

Pate, F.D., & Hutton, J.T. (1988). The use of soil chemistry data to address postmortem diagenesis in bone mineral. *Journal of Archaeological Science, 15,* 729–739.

Pate, F.D., Hutton, J.T., & Norrish, K. (1989). Ionic exchange between soil solution and bone: towards a predictive model. *Applied Geochemistry, 4,* 303–316.

Peirce, J.R. (1997). The biology of Australian weeds: 31. *Oxalis pes-caprae* L. *Plant Protection Quarterly, 12*(3), 110–119.

Pendick, D. (1998). Dig this. *New Scientist, September,* 34–37.

Pfeiffer, S., Milne, S., & Stevenson, R.M. (1998). The natural decomposition of adipocere. *Journal of Forensic Sciences, 43*(2), 368–370.

Pickering, R.B., & Bachman, D.C. (1997). *The use of forensic anthropology,* Boca Raton: CRC Press LLC.

Piepenbrink, H. (1986). Two examples of biogenous dead bone decomposition and their consequences for taphonomic interpretation. *Journal of Archaeological Sciences, 13,* 417–430.

Pinto, S., & Wilson, P. (1990). Serial murder. In *Trends and Issues in Crime and Criminal Justice* (No. 25). Canberra, Australia: Australian Institute of Criminology.

Powell, K. (2004). Detecting buried human remains using near-surface geophysical instruments. *Exploration Geophysics, 35*(1), 88–92.

Powell, K. (2006). *The detection of buried human skeletal remains in the Australian environment* (Unpublished PhD thesis). University of Adelaide, Australia.

Pringle, J.K., Jervis, J., Cassella, J.P., & Cassidy, N.J. (2008). Time-lapse geophysical investigations over a simulated urban clandestine grave. *Journal of Forensic Sciences, 53*(6), 1405–1416.

Queensland Police Service, (1999). *Police Dog Squad: human remains detection training manual* (unpublished manual).

Quigley, C. (1963). *The corpse: A history.* Appalachia, NC: McFarland & Co.

Radosevich, S.C. (1993). The six deadly sins of trace element analysis: A case of wishful thinking. In M. Sandford (Ed.), *Investigations of ancient human tissue: Chemical analyses in anthropology,* (pp. 269–332). Langhorne, PA: Gordon & Breach Science Publishers.

Rees, M., Condit, R., Crawley, M., Pacala, S., & Tilman, D. (2001). Long-term studies of vegetation dynamics. *Science, 293,* 650–654.

Reichs, K.J. (1992). Forensic Anthropology in the 1990s. *American Journal of Forensic Medicine and Pathology, 13*(2), 146–153.

Rentoul, E., & Smith, H. (1973). *Glaister's Medical Jurisprudence and Toxicology.* (13th ed.). Edinburgh: Churchill Livingstone.

Rodriguez, W., & Bass, W.M. (1985). Decomposition of buried bodies and methods that may aid in their location. *Journal of Forensic Sciences, 30*(3), 836–852.

Rowell, D.L. (1994). *Soil science: Methods and applications.* Essex, UK: Addison, Wesley, Longman.

Ruffell, A., McCabe, A., Donnelly, C., & Sloan, B. (2009). Location and assessment of an historic (150–160 years old) mass grave using geographic and ground penetrating radar investigation, NW Ireland. *Journal of Forensic Sciences, 54*(2), 382–394.

Sandford, M. (1993). Understanding the biogenic-diagenetic continuum: Interpreting elemental concentrations of archaeological bone. In M. Sandford (Ed.), *Investigations of ancient human tissue: Chemical analyses in anthropology* (pp. 1–48). Langhorne, PA: Gordon & Breach Science Publishers.

Scanvic, J. (1997). *Aerospatial remote sensing in geology.* Rotterdam/Brookfield: A.A. Balkema.

Schultz, J.J. (1997). *Microscopic Structure of Bone.* In W.D. Haglund & M.H. Sorg (Eds.), *Forensic taphonomy: The postmortem fate of human remains* (pp. 187–200). New York: CRC Press.

Schultz, J.J., Collins, M., & Falsetti, A. (2006). Sequential monitoring of burials containing large pig cadavers using ground penetrating radar. *Journal of Forensic Sciences, 51*(3), 607–616.

Schultz, J.J., Falsetti, A.B., Collins, M., Koppenjan, S.K., & Warren, M. (2002). *The detection of forensic burials in Florida using GPR.* Proceedings of the 9th International Conference of Ground Penetrating Radar, Santa Barbara, CA.

Schwartz, J.H. (1993). *What the bones tell us.* Tucson, AZ: The University of Arizona Press.

Scollar, I., Tabbagh, A., Hesse A., & Herzog, I. (1990). *Archaeological prospecting and remote sensing.* Cambridge: Cambridge University Press.

Skinner, M., & Lazenby, R.A. (1993). *Found! Human remains: A field manual for the discovery of the recent human skeleton.* Burnaby, Canada: Archaeology Press.

Snell, K.D.M. (2003). Gravestones, belonging and local attachment in England. *Past and Present, 179,* 97–134.

Spennemann, D.H.R., & Franke, B. (1995). Archaeological techniques for exhumations: A unique data source for crime scene investigations. *Forensic Science International, 74,* 5–15.

Spriggs, J.A. (1989). On and off-site conservation of bone. In C.A. Roberts, F. Lee & J. Bintiff (Eds.), *Burial archaeology: Current research, methods and developments* (pp. 39–45). Oxford: BAR British Series 211.

Stanley, J. M. (1983). Subsurface survey: The use of magnetics in Australian archaeology. In G. Connah (Ed.), *Australian field archaeology: A guide to techniques* (pp. 82–86). Canberra, Australia: Australian Institute of Aboriginal Studies.

Star, J.L., Estes, L.E., & McGuire, K.C. (Eds.) (1997). *Integration of geographic information systems and remote sensing.* Cambridge: Cambridge University Press.

Stewart, M. (1970). *The crystal cave.* New York: William Morrow.

Stott, P. (1996). Ground penetrating radar: A technique for investigating the burrow structures of fossorial vertebrates. *Wildlife Research, 23,* 519–530.

Strange, J. (2003). 'Tho' lost to sight, to memory dear': Pragmatism, sentimentality and working-class attitudes towards the grave, c.1875–1914. *Mortality, 8*(2), 144–159.

Swanton, B., & Wilson, P. (1989). Research brief: Missing persons. *Trends and Issues in Crime and Criminal Justice* (No. 17), Canberra, Australia: Australian Institute of Criminology.

Swigert, V.L., & Farrell, R.A. (1976). *Murder, inequality and the law: Differential treatment in the legal process.* Massachusetts, Toronto: Lexington Books.

Swindells, M. (1994). Remaining evidence. *Police Review, 7 October,* 14–15.

Thomas, D.G. 1999, Investigative sub-surface search: The pros and cons of some instrumented search technologies available to police in Australia. *Australian Police Journal, 53*(1), 62–72.

Thomas, P. (1995). *Talking bones: The science of forensic anthropology.* New York: Facts on File Inc.

Trueman, C.N., & Martill, D.M. (2002). The long-term survival of bone. *Archaeometry, 44*(3), 371–382.

Tolstoy, N. (1988). *The coming of the king.* London: Corgi Books.

Tuck, D. (1996). *A field guide to the detection and recovery of buried human remains.* NSW Police, Paper submitted for the Diploma in Applied Science in Forensic Investigation (NSW Police), Canberra Institute of Technology, Canberra, Australia.

Turner, B. & Wiltshire, P. (1999). Experimental validation of forensic evidence: A study of the decomposition of buried pigs in a heavy clay soil. *Forensic Science International, 101,* 113–122.

Ubelaker, D. (1997). Application of science. *International Police Review, Nov/Dec*, 30.

Ubelaker, D. (1978). *Human skeletal remains: Excavation, analysis, interpretation* (3rd ed.). Washington: Taraxacum.

Ubelaker, D., & Scammell, H. (1992), *Bones: A forensic detective's casebook.* New York: M. Evans & Company.

Unterberger, R.R. (1992). Ground penetrating radar finds disturbed earth over burials. *Fourth International Conference on Ground Penetrating Radar, Geological Survey of Finland, Special Paper 16*, 351–357.

Vass, A., Barshick, S., Sega, G., Caton, J., Skeen, J.T., Love, J.C., & Synstelien, J.A. (2002). Decomposition chemistry of human remains: A new methodology for determining the postmortem interval. *Journal of Forensic Sciences, 47*(3), 542–553.

Vass, A., Bass, W.M., Wolt, J.D., Foss, J.E., & Ammons, J.T. (1992). Time since death determinations of human cadavers using soil solution. *Journal of Forensic Sciences, 37*(5), 1236–1253.

Vass, A., Smith, R.R., Thompson, C.V., Burnett, M.N., Dulgerian, N., & Eckenrode, B.A. (2008). Odor analysis of decomposing buried human remains. *Journal of Forensic Sciences, 53*(2), 384–391.

Wakely, M. (2008). *Sweet sorrow: A beginner's guide to death.* Melbourne, Australia: Melbourne University Press.

Waldron, T. (1987). The potential of analysis of chemical constituents of bone. In A. Boddington, A.N. Garland & R.C. Janaway (Eds.), *Death, decay and reconstruction: Approaches to archaeology and forensic science* (pp. 149–162). Manchester, UK: Manchester University Press.

White, A. (2009, October 20). Forensic analysts review findings in Loleta case. *Times Standard.* Retrieved October 21, 2009 from http://www.times_standard.com.localnews/ci_13599713

Williams, M. (Ed.) (1969). *South Australia from the air.* Adelaide, Australia: Griffin Press.

Woolley, L. (1949). *Digging up the past.* Harmondsworth, UK: Penguin Books.

Wright, R. (1996). Uncovering genocide, war crimes: The archaeological evidence. *International Network on Holocaust and Genocide, 11*(3), 8–11.

Wu, A.H.B., & Bellantoni, N.F. (2003). Stability of cholesterol gall stones after 165 years of burial. *Journal of Forensic Sciences, 48*(3), 633–635.

Yoon, G.L., & Park, J.B. (2001). Sensitivity of leachate and fine contents on electrical resistivity variations of sandy soils. *Journal of Hazardous Materials, B84*, 147–161.

www.ingramcontent.com/pod-product-compliance
Lightning Source LLC
Chambersburg PA
CBHW041304210326
41598CB00005B/23